β

Gunfight!

GUNFIGHT!

Thirteen Western Stories
Edited by James C. Work

University of Nebraska Press
Lincoln and London

"The Reformation of Calliope" originally appeared in *Heart of the West* by O. Henry, 1904.

"Hopalong Sits In" by Clarence E. Mulford originally appeared in *Short Stories Magazine*, 10 January 1930.

"The Man Who Shot Liberty Valance" originally appeared in *Cosmopolitan*, July 1949. Copyright © 1949 by Dorothy M. Johnson, copyright © renewed 1977 by Dorothy M. Johnson. Reprinted by permission of McIntosh and Otis, Inc.

"Top Hand" by Luke Short originally appeared in the *Saturday Evening Post*, 30 October 1943. Reprinted with permission of the *Saturday Evening Post*, Kate Hirson, and Daniel Glidden.

"The Tin Star" originally appeared in *Colliers*, 6 December 1947. © John Cunningham 1947, renewed 1975.

"Massacre at Cottonwood Springs" by Lewis B. Patten first appeared in *Mammoth Western Magazine* (5/50). Copyright © 1950 by Ziff-Davis Publications, Inc. Copyright © 1978 by Lewis B. Patten. Reprinted by arrangement with Golden West Literary Agency. All rights reserved.

"The Last Shot" originally appeared in *Esquire*, 1949. © Frank O'Rourke. Reprinted by permission of Edith Carlson.

"The Guns of William Longley" by Donald Hamilton appeared in *Iron Men and Silver Stars*, Fawcett, 1967.

"The Death of Sun" was first published in *Cosmopolitan*, October 1972. Copyright © 1972 by William Eastlake. Reprinted by permission of the author.

"The Fastest Gun" is from *Great American Guns* and *Frontier Fighters* by Will Bryant, published by Grosset & Dunlap, New York, 1961. Reprinted by permission of the author.

"Cowboys" originally appeared in *Okies* by Gerald Haslam (1973). Reprinted by permission of the author.

"Righteous Guns" appeared in *The Best Western Stories of Bill Pronzini*, ed. Bill Pronzini and Martin H. Greenberg. Copyright 1990 by Bill Pronzini. Reprinted by permission of the author.

"The Field" by Mark Holden originally appeared in *Southwest Review* 69, no. 4 (autumn 1984). Reprinted by permission of the author.

© 1996 by the University of Nebraska Press
All rights reserved
Manufactured in the United States of America
⊗ The paper in this book meets the minimum
requirements of American National Standard
for Information Sciences—Permanence of
Paper for Printed Library Materials,
ANSI Z39.48-1984.
Library of Congress Cataloging-in-Publication Data
Gunfight! : thirteen western stories /
edited by James C. Work.
p. cm.
ISBN 0-8032-4780-X
(cl : alk. paper)
1. Western stories. 2. American fiction—
West (U.S.) 3. West (U.S.)—
Social life and customs—Fiction.
I. Work, James C.
PS648.W4G79 1996
813'.087408—dc20 95-26569
CIP

Contents

Acknowledgments

Making this book brought many good moments for me. Each discovery of some little fact, each flash of insight about a story, each new connection served to reward me for a few hours of reading and research. But the very best moments came from being in touch with the people who helped it all happen.

Each week, the mail brought letters from the authors who wanted to help: Gerald Haslam, suggesting stories by friends even when he knew I might prefer one of those over his; John Cunningham, Will Bryant, and Bill Pronzini, sending me accurate information as well as more gunfight anecdotes; Mark Holden, writing to say, "I don't know what you're up to, but you can use my story"; and John Jakes, exchanging letters with me even though I didn't use his story.

The weekly mail also brought the contributions from Phyllis Doughman, who spent uncountable hours searching library collections for more stories. Out of the thirty or forty that we found, more than half were her discoveries. Of the final thirteen, she deserves credit for at least six—seven, if you count the one I wanted to omit and that she insisted on saving. Phyllis also researched the lives of the writers, wrote twelve of the biographical sketches for this book, and acted as critic and sounding board for my introduction and commentaries.

The biographical sketch of Frank O'Rourke was written by Edith Carlson.

All of us—writers and collaborating editors—need to thank Bill Regier for his good humor and supreme patience and most of all for his enthusiasm over the project. His encouragement has made all the difference.

Introduction

Textbooks call the West an arid region, but to most Westerners it's just plain dry. According to one story about it, two expectant fathers were sitting outside the delivery room, one of them a long-time prairie farmer and the other recently from the East. The doctor came out and told them that they were both new fathers. The Easterner's newborn weighed eight and one-half pounds, but the Westerner's weighed only a pound.

"What a shame," the Easterner said. "All those months of waiting, and all your wife's labor, and the child only weighs a pound."

"Aw, that's okay," the Westerner drawled. "Hell, out here we're lucky just to get our seed back."

The seeds for this book were planted about twenty years ago when a well-meaning colleague of mine talked our library's special collections curator into buying up all the postwar pulp western magazines he could get his hands on. Acquiring these masterpieces turned out to be relatively easy and inexpensive; the paper was of the cheap pulp variety that would disintegrate after about twenty-five years, meaning that most owners were anxious to sell before their investments started turning into weevil forage. As I discovered, the writing in those magazines was about as bad as the paper it was printed on.

I had just come into the field of western American literature after a decade of Victorian English poetry, and I was finding western literature a little arid when it came to research topics. My ambition to become a published instructor attracted the attention of my colleague, the collector. He was anxious to justify the acquisition of pulp western magazines and eager to have me (or anybody) begin working on them before they became confetti.

I began a dutiful perusal of the pulps, gingerly handling the dry volumes and trying not to get dust up my nose. One good sneeze would vaporize the pages in front of me, and the more I saw the more convinced I was that a sneeze wouldn't do any good: what the collection needed was a moderate tornado.

I managed to breathe through my mouth long enough to study about a hundred and fifty of the fragile, yellowed magazines, most of them dating from the 1940s and 1950s. The titles included *Ace-High Western Stories*, *Western Action*, *.44 Western*, *Popular Western*, *Double Action Western*, and *Two Gun Western Novels*. Not very promising for a young intellectual hoping to write a scholarly article about American literature. You could read most of these magazines while watching Monday night football and never lose track of the score. Among the hundreds of writers, only three names were familiar: Zane Grey, Luke Short, and Louis L'Amour. The academic potential of this stuff seemed to be drying up even faster than the old yellow pages, and I started wondering if a fake fit of sneezing would be enough to get me thrown out of the special collections room forever.

Then I noticed something that was eventually to lead me to stories of better quality: every cover illustration on each of those hundred and fifty story treasuries showed a man holding a gun. No matter what else or who else was in the picture, there was a man holding a gun. He was never holding a hammer, or a bucket, or a guitar, or a book, or anything else. Always a gun.

Even more interesting, each of the gun-pointers was pictured as some kind of cowboy, complete with cowboy hat, cowboy shirt, cowboy bandanna, and cowboy shave and haircut. An obvious fact dawned on me: illustrators used the image of the gun and the image of the cowboy in order to sell magazines.

I may have been new to western American literature, but as a third generation Westerner I knew a little about cowboys and livestock. Around herds of range cattle, a careless shot from a cowboy's revolver could stampede a whole week's work and leave hoof tracks all along his spine. It also could put a hole through his boot and through anything that might be in his boot, such as his foot. A stray shot could put a hole through anything in the vicinity, such as a foreman, who might then decide to pick up a singletree and re-shape the pistolero's skull with it.

More than half of the pulp western illustrations showed buildings in the background, indicating that the pistol-pointing cowboy was spending the day in town. Here again, the picture of a cowboy blasting away with his single-action struck me as being a little less than logical. When a herder could get away from the herd long enough to ride into town, he considered it a treat and a privilege; he was there to have a good time, not to use the residents for target practice. Whipping out the ol' sidearm in public was a good way to get his best go-to-town clothes perforated by the local constable.

This pulp magazine image of the gunslinger cowboy and the good guy–

bad guy gunfight looked like seed material to me. I began to see some research questions here. First, who started this idea of writing stories about cowboy gunfighters? Second, why do gunfights seem to sell so many books, magazines, and films? And third, are there gunfight stories out there that don't follow the familiar formula?

To the first question—where did the western gunfight story begin?—the answer came easily: in *The Virginian*, published in 1902. There had been plenty of shooting in earlier pulp fiction, mostly in the pages of Beadle's dime novels and cheap imitations of Beadle's. The first of the Beadle books was written in 1860 by Ann Sophia Winterbotham Stephens and was titled *Malaeska: Indian Wife of the White Hunter*. The craze for mass-produced works of mayhem reached a high point in about 1881, when Beadle's contract with the printer called for sixty thousand copies of each edition of a book, and dozens of books went through ten or more editions. The demand dropped off slowly as pulps began to cost more and kept offering less original material. Beadle's was out of business by 1920.

The works published by Beadle, written by such authors as Ned Buntline, were strictly entertainment, strictly thrillers. Owen Wister's *The Virginian*, on the other hand, was a "real" novel that introduced the prototype of the walk-down, get-out-of-town gunfight. Wister took his hero as seriously as he took the West, granting his novel a historical dimension by basing it on Wyoming's Johnson County War of 1892. The Virginian and a man named Trampas have developed a lethal dislike for each other, and as the book nears its climax Trampas finally manages to say the wrong thing to the Virginian. It is a statement that soon became a standard feature of western books and movies:

"Your friends have saved your life. I'll give you until sundown to leave town," says Trampas.

The gunfight soon follows—at about sundown, which for some reason seems to surprise Trampas more than it surprises the reader—but Wister's description of it seems pretty tame. In fact, you might have to read it twice to realize that the "wind" the Virginian feels going past his arm was caused by fifty grains of black powder and a .45 slug.

"It is quite a while after sunset," he heard himself say.

A wind seemed to blow his sleeve off his arm, and he replied to it, and saw Trampas pitch forward. He saw Trampas raise his arm from the ground and fall again, and lie there this time, still. A little smoke was rising from the pistol on the ground, and he looked at his own, and saw the smoke flowing upward out of it.

"I expect that's all," he said aloud. But as he came nearer Trampas, he covered him with his weapon. He stopped a moment, seeing the hand on the ground move. Two fingers twitched, and then ceased; for it was all.

That's it. That's the prototype gunfight in western American literature. It is short and understated, and the Virginian and Trampas are not even gunslingers. They are just cowboys. Granted, Trampas spends most of his time accumulating livestock by dishonest means, and the Virginian spends most of his time courting the eastern school mistress. But they are still supposed to be cowboys. Not gunfighters.

The Virginian poses a problem, you see. Cover illustrations on pulp westerns indicate that gunfights sell the fiction. So when Wister wrote about courtship and cattle theft and card games and humor contests, he was wasting his time. More than one and a half million copies of *The Virginian* were sold by the time Wister died in 1938. But apparently more could have been sold just by having various ranch employees hold daily shootouts with the local American Federation of Stagecoach Bandits and Steer Stealers.

Many western writers took Wister's example to heart and began incorporating the main-street showdown in their own stories. It became a standard device—so standard that literary critic Bernard DeVoto said it "has kept the cowboy story from becoming serious fiction." If it wasn't for the glamour of the walk-down, shootout fantasy, he said, we would have far fewer of these gunpowder romances and more stories dealing with other important parts of cowboy life in the West.

Where is the appeal? It might be in the mystique of the American cowboy himself, since the gunfight and the cowboy are so closely linked. The cowboy of formula fiction and film, who is seldom seen actually working with cattle, is a romantic hero. He is independent, chivalrous, self-sufficient, skilled, and strong. Many writers liked to portray him as a kind of freelance lone ranger, protecting citizens and capturing criminals on the lawless frontier. When this mythical figure gets into a gunfight, it becomes a contest between good and evil.

Another reason for the appeal of gunfight stories might be historical accuracy. I have had avid readers of westerns tell me that westerns are a good way to learn history. That's fine, except that pulps and horse operas are seldom historically "accurate." Gunfights resembling the fictional ones probably happened in the frontier West (although Jack Schaefer, the author of *Shane*, once offered a cash reward to anyone who could bring him documented proof of an actual walk-down). But you would not buy a copy of *.44 Western* or a ticket to see *High Noon* in order to learn the facts. Fiction and film romanticized the whole idea of a shootout and led the public to believe that any two Westerners who took a dislike to each other were likely to draw their Colts and cut loose.

The Virginian suggests a few other reasons why readers like western gunfights. Simplicity, for example; there is little or no ambiguity about the shootout in which the Virginian kills Trampas. Trampas is a thief and a backshooter who has insulted the schoolteacher and slandered the Virginian and now invites the hero to do something about it. The Virginian is forced into the gunfight, and the gunfight settles it once and for all. We find the same thing in *Shane* and in Larry McMurtry's *Lonesome Dove* and in hundreds of other tales: the shootout, which is unambiguous and inevitable, will put an end to all shootouts. Many of us live in a world of mixed motives where nothing ever seems to get decided. Values shift and change. The bad guys always manage to avoid punishment. In the Virginian's world, everyone knows who the backshooting crook is and everyone appreciates the Virginian for dropping the hammer on him.

Gunfights such as the one in *The Virginian* might also appeal to readers because they are duels. Duels have been part of literature since Hector and Achilles tossed spears at each other by the walls of Troy. Readers have always liked duels, whether they involve Greek heroes or Robin Hood or the Three Musketeers. The blackpowder party in *The Virginian* looks like a duel. Honor is often the issue in a traditional duel, and the Virginian explains to his fiancée that this is a question of honor. In the literary tradition it is aristocrats who do the dueling. More than once, Wister calls his cowboy hero a "natural aristocrat."

It was beginning to look as if I could harvest something here. I had a promising hypothesis: in western fiction, an ancient literary tradition is continued when characters in cowboy hats (who aren't necessarily cowboys) reenact that male bonding ritual affectionately known as a duel to the death.

Wrong hypothesis. A gunfight and a duel are not the same thing.

In the Middle Ages, two noblemen wearing steel armor and carrying what they hoped were armor-piercing lances charged at each other on horses. Or they hacked at each other with heavy swords or axes.

Later, in the seventeenth and eighteenth centuries, upper-crust champions faced off with rapiers or single-shot pistols, which represented a step toward safer dueling conditions. The fencing sword became lighter and easier to handle, but it also became more fragile. This meant that your opponent was more careful about trying to beat you to death with it, and more likely to slice you into thin pieces. The dueling pistols of that era, with unpredictable powder and soft lead balls distorted from being hammered down the barrel, were rarely accurate beyond twenty paces.

Speaking of such pistols reminds me that the Virginian's namesake state was the center of a culture in which American duels did take place among some of America's aristocratic gentry. Andrew Jackson's killing of Charles Dickinson in an 1806 duel in Kentucky enhanced his reputation as a man of principles. This came two years after the famed Hamilton-Burr duel in Virginia, an encounter that illustrates the difference between dueling and shooting it out.

The pistols of that duel, I should add, evidently had a mystique of their own. They belonged to John Barker Church, a friend of the Hamilton family; designed for dueling, they were relatively short, blocky-looking single shot percussion pistols with heavy barrels and small bores. X-ray photographs made during the 1970s revealed that the Church pistols had hidden hair trigger mechanisms, so the person who knew the secret of the mechanism could get off a shot slightly faster than could the opponent.

In 1797 Alexander Hamilton borrowed these pistols when he challenged James Monroe, but at the last minute the antagonists settled their argument nonviolently. John Church exchanged shots with Aaron Burr in a 1799 duel, but the only casualty was Burr's heavy overcoat, which sustained a serious hole. Hamilton's son Philip used the Church pistols in a duel with a lawyer named Eacker in 1801 and was killed. And the most famous duel, again with the Church pistols, was in 1804 when Aaron Burr killed Hamilton. According to some eyewitness accounts, Hamilton's pistol went off as he was bringing it down and clipped a tree branch high over Burr's head. Burr took more time for his shot.

Such weapons as the Church pistols, like fencing swords, were owned by upper-class persons and were used primarily in formal semiprivate exchanges. In the nineteenth-century American West, a serious social encounter of the disagreeable sort was likely to bring out the six-cylinder repeating revolver; behind it would be an ordinary citizen (such as a cowboy) who might or might not be on polite speaking terms with the person at whom he was shooting.

On the American frontier of the 1800s, revolvers were tools used by working men. In Europe it took wealth and free time to practice fencing or shooting; on the frontier virtually anybody with a paycheck could afford to buy a revolver, and any fool could point it and pull the trigger six times. The shooting might be accurate, but that wouldn't indicate whether the sharpshooter was an aristocrat or a saddle tramp.

Duels and gunfights also differ in motive. On the American frontier, shootings generally involved either the defense of life or a question about property. In firsthand accounts by Theodore Roosevelt, Andy Adams, and Emerson Hough, we find most of the shooting being done either by defenders of home, hearth, or herd, or by drunks. Some men exchanged Peacemaker pleasantries in the name of "justice," but few actual gun battles were fought over matters of pride, passion, honor, or upper-class prerogative. Some unreconstructed Southern gentlemen and army officers had "affairs of honor," but these were few and far between.

In *The Duel* (1970) Robert Baldick quotes an 1894 work by Bronson Howard: "If there is any such thing as an 'American' duel, it is what is familiarly known as 'shooting on sight'. The challenger sends word to his enemy that he will shoot him the next time he sees him, and thereupon the latter arms himself and takes his walks abroad with much caution, until the two meet, when both begin a brisk fusillade with their revolvers, and one of them is usually killed, together with from four to six of the bystanders."

From my pulp magazine "research" I had figured out that western literature gunfights do not necessarily involve cowboys, and that American writers were not just imitating the European dueling tradition. I also learned that I could hold a sneeze for twenty minutes before my eyes began to go blurry.

Eventually, after reading hundreds of examples, I also recognized the single most important characteristic of the western-style shootout. It dates back to *The Virginian*, where Trampas's defeat dramatizes Owen Wister's concept of democracy. This same concept, with its many variations, is more likely than gore and violence to attract readers. As a selling point, it probably succeeds better than any other single factor, including the promise of authentic historical description. Consciously or subconsciously, whether in cowboy fiction or detective fiction or even science fiction, American readers expect the outcome of a gun battle to confirm the democratic principle of equal opportunity through the victory of the better character. Wister summarized it in chapter 12 of *The Virginian*: "We had seen little men artificially held up in high places, and great men artificially held down in low places, and our own justice-loving hearts abhorred this violence to human nature. . . . We acknowledged and gave freedom to true aristocracy, saying "Let the best man win, whoever he is." Let the best man win! That is America's word. That is true democracy. And true democracy and true aristocracy are one and the same thing" (147).

The Virginian and the schoolmarm argue the question of whether all men are created equal. The Virginian believes in a natural social scale among people, that some individual human beings are just naturally better than others. "A man has got to prove himself my equal before I'll believe him," says the Virginian. Trampas sets out to do just that—and the result is, well, *democratic*.

The chance to show who is the better man: that is the common factor I discovered in the pulp western magazines and dime western novels and formula western movies. I am not forgetting, however, that I am dealing with fiction. In reality, frontier Americans seldom exchanged lead as a way of establishing their relative position on the social scale. More frequently, they resorted to gunfire to make a point about property ownership or to demonstrate their degree of intoxication. But reality makes for dull entertainment, and so the lurid, romantic magazine covers promised something to go along with the fast-paced action and the buckskin Sir Galahad. Those cover illustrations assured the reader that once upon a time, somewhere in the mythic West, all the average person needed for equality and self-sufficiency was a little skill with a good revolver. And in most of those pictures it was a single-action Colt.

"The Equalizer" was its nickname, although it was also called the "Peacemaker" and the "Frontier" in its various models. Colt's Patent Fire Arms Manufacturing Company, Inc., began producing it in 1873 as the "Model P" .45 caliber centerfire six-shot single-action revolver. Today, long after the need for such a weapon has disappeared, several versions of it are still being manufactured. The bullets, forty-five hundredths of an inch in diameter, feel heavy and serious. The plow-handle shape of the grip fits the hand as if molded to it. When being cocked to fire, the Colt makes three clicks that have a distinctive and authoritative sound. Millions of people have seen this firearm, mostly in movies or on magazine covers, and for the majority of film and fiction fans, it symbolizes one concept above all others: America's legendary frontier offered people opportunity and democracy, but it was the frontier six-shooter that offered them equality.

As I learned more about Western literature, I agreed more with Bernard DeVoto's opinion. Too many second-rate writers had tried to imitate the fight between Trampas and the Virginian, until it turned into a formula. Too often, the formula became the whole story and the suspense and excitement were lost. All the stories began to sound alike: there's a good guy and a bad guy and they don't like each other and the bad guy does something really bad and the good guy shoots him. End of story.

That realization was also to be the end of my pulp western research. I handed in my respirator and accepted an offer to help assemble a new edition of Jack Schaefer's *Shane*. After that, I spent a few years working on an anthology of western American literature, and I more or less forgot about gunfights in fiction. But a few years ago, during the annual meeting of the Western Literature Association, I was participating in the yearly Jim Beam Memorial Seminar on World Problems. I began holding forth on the topic of how gunfights have ruined western fiction. I said that there *should* be some non-formula, good-quality shootout material out there somewhere. A colleague took me seriously and later began mailing stories to me. About half of the stories in this collection came to me that way.

That volunteer colleague was also willing to do a biography of each writer, and for each selection I added a brief commentary. Each writer you find in these pages has a uniquely interesting background, and each story has its own surprise twist on the idea of a shootout. Some of this fiction is humorous, some of it is action-packed and graphic, and some of it is thought-provoking. Much of it illustrates that there is a mystique to having a six-shooter in the hand, some undefinable power the pistol has to change a man's image of himself. And whether written in 1907 or in 1990, each story takes us to a different and unexpected perspective on the American notion of equality.

What I like best about our collection is that these stories are good literature. They show, in a small way, that the arid West produces more than dried-up formulas and worn-out stereotypes. Year after year for almost a century, we have been getting bumper crops of fiction. And even in the worst years, we still get our seed back.

Gunfight!

O. Henry
(William Sidney Porter)
1862–1910

Many western fiction writers have led pretty ordinary lives. The personal life of William S. Porter, however, rivaled those of his fictional characters. Before he had written his first story, the man who would adopt the O. Henry pen name had worked in Texas as a clerk and bookkeeper, a draftsman, a bank teller, and a newspaper journalist. When suddenly summoned back to Austin to face charges of embezzlement by the bank where he had worked, he decided to "go on the lam" and headed for New Orleans.

From New Orleans he worked his way to the British Honduras and later traveled through South America in the company of two train robbers, hiding out with an illicit cache of $30,000. Fate, however, caught up with him: he spent three years and three months in the Ohio State Penitentiary.

While serving his prison sentence, William Porter began to write short stories. After prison he decided to move to New York City to see if he could become a full-time fiction writer. It turned out, of course, that he could: his stories quickly made him an immensely popular author. Today, many have heard of O. Henry but few realize that he wrote so many westerns. Even fewer readers know that in *The Caballero's Way* he created the Cisco Kid, the same character who became a film hero to adolescent would-be cowboys around the world.

Most of O. Henry's western stories are collected in *The Heart of the West*. Modern literary critics discredit much of his work for being melodramatic and written according to predictable formulas, but his depictions of ranch life in early Texas are undeniably authentic. And he is unique among American writers for one thing: his pen name became an adjective in book reviews. Because of his clever twists of plot, reviewers who find a surprise at the end of a good book or story often say that it has an "O. Henry ending."

The Reformation of Calliope

Calliope Catesby was in his humors again. Ennui was upon him. This goodly promontory, the earth—particularly that portion of it known as Quicksand—was to him no more than a pestilent congregation of vapors. Overtaken by the megrims, the philosopher may seek relief in soliloquy; my lady find solace in tears; the flaccid Easterner scold at the millinery bills of his women folk. Such recourse was insufficient to the denizens of Quicksand. Calliope, especially, was wont to express his ennui according to his lights.

Over night Calliope had hung out signals of approaching low spirits. He had kicked his own dog on the porch of the Occidental Hotel, and refused to apologize. He had become capricious and fault-finding in conversation. While strolling about he reached often for twigs of mesquite and chewed the leaves fiercely. That was always an ominous act. Another symptom alarming to those who were familiar with the different stages of his doldrums was his increasing politeness and a tendency to use formal phrases. A husky softness succeeded the usual penetrating drawl in his tones. A dangerous courtesy marked his manners. Later, his smile became crooked, the left side of his mouth slanting upward, and Quicksand got ready to stand from under.

At this stage Calliope generally began to drink. Finally, about midnight, he was seen going homeward, saluting those whom he met with exaggerated but inoffensive courtesy. Not yet was Calliope's melancholy at the danger point. He would seat himself at the window of the room he occupied over Silvester's tonsorial parlor and there chant lugubrious and tuneless ballads until morning, accompanying the noises by appropriate maltreatment of a jingling guitar. More magnanimous than Nero, he would thus give musical warning of the forthcoming municipal upheaval that Quicksand was scheduled to endure.

A quiet, amiable man was Calliope Catesby at other times—quiet to indolence, and amiable to worthlessness. At best he was a loafer and a nuisance; at worst he was the Terror of Quicksand. His ostensible occupation was something subordinate in the real estate line; he drove the beguiled Easterner in buckboards out to look over lots and ranch property. Originally he came from one of the Gulf States, his lank six feet, slurring rhythm of speech, and sectional idioms giving evidence of his birthplace.

And yet, after taking on Western adjustments, this languid pine-box whittler, cracker barrel hugger, shady corner lounger of the cotton fields and sumac hills of the South became famed as a bad man among men who had made a life-long study of the art of truculence.

At nine the next morning Calliope was fit. Inspired by his own barbarous melodies and the contents of his jug, he was ready primed to gather fresh laurels from the diffident brow of Quicksand. Encircled and criss-crossed with cartridge belts, abundantly garnished with revolvers, and copiously drunk, he poured forth into Quicksand's main street. Too chivalrous to surprise and capture a town by silent sortie, he paused at the nearest corner and emitted his slogan—that fearful, brassy yell, so reminiscent of the steam piano, that has gained for him the classic appellation that had superseded his own baptismal name. Following close upon his vociferation came three shots from his forty-five by way of limbering up the guns and testing his aim. A yellow dog, the personal property of Colonel Swazey, the proprietor of the Occidental, fell feet upward in the dust with one farewell yelp. A Mexican who was crossing the street from the Blue Front grocery, carrying in his hand a bottle of kerosene, was stimulated to a sudden and admirable burst of speed, still grasping the neck of the shattered bottle. The new gilt weathercock on Judge Riley's lemon and ultra-marine two-story residence shivered, flapped, and hung by a splinter, the sport of the wanton breezes.

The artillery was in trim. Calliope's hand was steady. The high, calm ecstasy of habitual battle was upon him, though slightly embittered by the sadness of Alexander in that his conquests were limited to the small world of Quicksand.

Down the street went Calliope, shooting right and left. Glass fell like hail; dogs vamosed; chickens flew, squawking; feminine voices shrieked concernedly to youngsters at large. The din was perforated at intervals by the *staccato* of the Terror's guns, and was drowned periodically by the brazen screech that Quicksand knew so well. The occasion of Calliope's low spirits were legal holidays in Quicksand. All along the main street in advance of his coming clerks were putting up shutters and closing doors. Business would languish for a space. The right of way was Calliope's, and as he advanced, observing the dearth of opposition and the few opportunities for distraction, his ennui perceptibly increased.

But some four squares farther down lively preparations were being made to minister to Mr. Catesby's love for interchange of compliments and repartee. On the previous night numerous messengers had hastened to advise Buck Patterson, the city marshal, of Calliope's impending eruption. The patience of that official, often strained in extending leniency toward the disturber's misdeeds, had been overtaxed. In Quicksand some indulgence was accorded the natural ebullition of human nature. Providing that the lives of the more useful citizens were not recklessly squandered, or too much property needlessly laid waste, the community sentiment was against a too strict enforcement of the law. But Calliope had raised the limit. His outbursts had been too frequent and too violent to come within the classification of a normal and sanitary relaxation of spirit.

Buck Patterson had been expecting and awaiting in his little ten-by-twelve frame office that preliminary yell announcing that Calliope was feeling blue. When the signal came the City Marshal rose to his feet and buckled on his guns. Two deputy sheriffs and three citizens who had proven the edible qualities of fire also stood up, ready to bandy with Calliope's leaden jocularities.

"Gather that fellow in," said Buck Patterson, setting for the lines of the campaign. "Don't have no talk, but shoot as soon as you can get a show. Keep behind cover and bring him down. He's a nogood 'un. It's up to Calliope to turn up his toes this time, I reckon. Go to him all spraddled out, boys. And don't git too reckless, for what Calliope shoots at he hits."

Buck Patterson, tall, muscular, and solemn-faced, with his bright "City Marshal" badge shining on the breast of his blue flannel shirt, gave his posse directions for the onslaught upon Calliope. The plan was to accomplish the downfall of the Quicksand Terror without loss to the attacking party, if possible.

The splenetic Calliope, unconscious of retributive plots, was steaming down the channel, cannonading on either side, when he suddenly became aware of breakers ahead. The City Marshal and one of the deputies rose up behind some dry-goods boxes half a square to the front and opened fire. At the same time the rest of the posse, divided, shelled him from two side streets up which they were cautiously manoeuvring from a well-executed detour.

The first volley broke the lock of one of Calliope's guns, cut a neat underbit in his right ear, and exploded a cartridge in his crossbelt, scorching his ribs as it burst. Feeling braced up by this unexpected tonic to his spiritual depression, Calliope executed a *fortissimo* note from his upper registers, and returned the fire like an echo. The upholders of the law dodged at his flash, but a trifle too late to save one of the deputies a bullet just above the elbow, and the marshal a bleeding cheek from a splinter that a ball tore from a box he had ducked behind.

And now Calliope met the enemy's tactics in kind. Choosing with a rapid eye the street from which the weakest and least accurate fire had come, he invaded it at a double-quick, abandoning the unprotected middle of the street. With rare cunning the opposing force in that direction—one of the deputies and two of the valorous volunteers—waited, concealed by beer barrels, until Calliope had passed their retreat, and then peppered him from the rear. In another moment they were reinforced by the marshal and his other men, and then Calliope felt that in order to successfully prolong the delights of the controversy he must find some means of reducing the great odds against him. His eye fell upon a structure that seemed to hold out this promise, providing he could reach it.

Not far away was the little railroad station, its building a strong box house, ten by twenty feet, resting upon a platform four feet above ground. Windows were in each of its walls. Something like a fort it might become to a man thus sorely pressed by superior numbers.

Calliope made a bolt and rapid spurt for it, the marshal's crowd "smoking" him as he ran. He reached the haven in safety, the station agent leaving the building by a window, like a flying squirrel, as the garrison entered the door.

Patterson and his supporters halted under protection of a pile of lumber and held consultations. In the station was an unterrified desperado who was an excellent shot and carried an abundance of ammunition. For thirty yards on each side of the besieged was a stretch of bare, open ground. It was a sure thing that the man who attempted to enter that unprotected area would be stopped by one of Calliope's bullets.

The City Marshal was resolved. He had decided that Calliope Catesby should no more wake the echoes of Quicksand with his strident whoop. He had so announced. Officially and personally he felt imperatively bound to put the soft pedal on that instrument of discord. It played bad tunes.

Standing near was a hand truck used in the manipulation of small freight. It stood by a shed full of sacked wool, a consignment from one of the sheep ranches. On this truck the marshal and his men piled three heavy sacks of wool. Stooping low, Buck Patterson started for Calliope's fort, slowly pushing this loaded truck before him for protection. The posse, scattering broadly, stood ready to nip the besieged in case he should show himself in an effort to repel the juggernaut of justice that was creeping upon him. Only once did Calliope make demonstration. He fired from a window and soft tufts of wool spurted from the marshal's trustworthy bulwark. The return shots from the posse pattered against the window frame of the fort. No loss resulted on either side.

The marshal was too deeply engrossed in steering his protected battle-ship to be aware of the approach of the morning train until he was within a few feet of the platform. The train was coming up on the other side of it. It stopped only one minute at Quicksand. What an opportunity it would offer to Calliope! He had only to step out the other door, mount the train, and away.

Abandoning his breastworks, Buck, with his gun ready, dashed up the steps and into the room, driving open the closed door with one heave of his weighty shoulder. The members of the posse heard one shot fired inside, and then there was silence.

At length the wounded man opened his eyes. After a blank space he again could see and hear and feel and think. Turning his eyes about, he found himself lying on a wooden bench. A tall man with a perplexed countenance, wearing a big badge with "City Marshal" engraved upon it, stood over him. A little old woman in black, with a wrinkled face and sparkling black eyes, was holding a wet handkerchief against one of his temples. He was trying to get these facts fixed in his mind and connected with past events, when the old woman began to talk.

"There now, great, big, strong man! That bullet never tetched ye! Jest skeeted along the side of your head and sort of paralyzed ye for a spell. I've heerd of sech things afor! con-cussion is what they names it. Abel Wadkins used to kill squirrels that way—barkin' em, Abe called it. You jest been barked, sir, and you'll be all right in a little bit. Feel lots better already, don't ye! You just lay still a while longer and let me bathe your head. You don't know me, I reckon, and 'tain't surprisin' that you shouldn't. I come in on that train from Alabama to see my son. Big son, ain't he? Lands! you wouldn't hardly think he'd ever been a baby, would ye? This is my son, sir."

Half turning, the old woman looked up at the standing man, her worn face lighting with a proud and wonderful smile. She reached out one veined and calloused hand and took one of her son's. Then smiling cheerily down at the prostrate man, she continued to dip the handkerchief in the waiting-room tin washbasin and gently apply it to his temple. She had the benevolent garrulity of old age.

"I ain't seen my son before," she continued, "in eight years. One of my nephews, Elkanah Price, he's a conductor on one of them railroads, and he got me a pass to come out here. I can stay a whole week on it, and then it'll take me back again. Jest think, now, that little boy of mine has got to be a officer—a city marshal of a whole town! That's something like a constable, ain't it? I never knowed he was a officer; he didn't say nothin' about it in his letters. I reckon he thought this old mother'd be skeered about the danger he was in. But, laws! I never was much of a hand to git skeered. 'Tain't no use. I heard them guns a-shootin' while I was gittin' off them cars, and I see smoke a-comin' out of the depot, but I jest walked right along. Then I see son's face lookin' out through the window. I know him at onect. He met me at the door, and squeezed me 'most to death. And there you was, sir, a-lyin' there jest like you was dead, and I 'lowed we'd see what might be done to help sot you up."

"I think I'll sit up now," said the concussion patient. "I'm feeling pretty fair by this time."

He sat, somewhat weakly yet, leaning against the wall. He was a rugged man, big-boned and straight. His eyes, steady and keen, seemed to linger upon the face of the man standing so still above him. His look wandered often from the face he studied to the marshal's badge upon the other's breast.

"Yes, yes, you'll be all right," said the old woman, patting his arm, "if you don't get to cuttin' up agin, and havin' folks shootin' at you. Son told me about you, sir, while you was layin' senseless on the floor. Don't you take it as meddlesome fer an old woman with a son as big as you to talk about it. And you mustn't hold no grudge ag'in my son for havin' to shoot at ye. A officer has got to take up for the law—it's his duty—and them that acts bad and lives wrong has to suffer. Don't blame my son any, sir—'tain't his fault. He's always been a good boy—good when he was growin' up, and kind and 'bedient and well-behaved. Won't you let me advise you, sir, not to do so no more? Be a good man, and leave liquor alone and live peaceably and godly. Keep away from bad company and work honest and sleep sweet."

The black-mittened hand of the old pleader gently touched the breast of the man she addressed. Very earnest and candid her old, worn face looked. In her rusty black dress and antique bonnet she sat, near the close of a long life, and epitomized the experience of the world. Still the man to whom she spoke gazed above her head, contemplating the silent son of the old mother.

"What does the marshal say?" he asked. "Does he believe the advice is good? Suppose the marshal speaks up and says if the talk's right?"

The tall man moved uneasily. He fingered the badge on his breast for a moment, and then he put an arm around the old woman and drew her close to him. She smiled the unchanging mother smile of three-score years, and patted his big brown hand with her crooked, mittened fingers while her son spake.

"I say this," he said, looking squarely into the eyes of the other man, "that if I was in your place I'd follow it. If I was a drunken, desp'rate character, without shame or hope, I'd follow it. If I was in your place and you was in mine I'd say: "Marshal, I'm willin' to swear if you'll give me the chance I'll quit the racket. I'll drop the tanglefoot and the gun play, and won't play hoss no more. I'll be a good citizen and go to work and quit my foolishness. So help me God!" That's what I'd say to you if you was marshal and I was in your place."

"Hear my son talkin'," said the old woman softly. "Hear him, sir. You promise to be good and he won't do you no harm. Forty-one year ago his heart first beat ag'in mine, and it's beat true ever since."

The other man rose to his feet, trying his limbs and stretching his muscles.

"Then," said he, "if you was in my place and said that, and I was marshal, I'd say: "Go free, and do your best to keep your promise.""

"Lawsy!" exclaimed the old woman, in a sudden flutter, "ef I didn't clear forget that trunk of mine! I see a man settin' it on the platform jest as I seen son's face in the window, and it went plum out of my head. There's eight jars of home-made quince jam in that trunk that I made myself. I wouldn't have nothin' happen to them jars for a red apple."

Away to the door she trotted, spry and anxious, and then Calliope Catesby spoke out to Buck Patterson:

"I just couldn't help it, Buck. I seen her through the window a-comin' in. She had never heard a word 'bout my tough ways. I didn't have the nerve to let her know I was a worthless cuss bein' hunted down by the community. There you was lyin' where my shot laid you, like you was dead. The idea struck me sudden, and I just took your badge off and fastened it onto myself, and I fastened my reputation onto you. I told her I was the marshal and you was a holy terror. You can take your badge back now, Buck."

With shaking fingers Calliope began to unfasten the disc of metal from his shirt.

"Easy there!" said Buck Patterson. "You keep that badge right where it is, Calliope Catesby. Don't you dare to take it off till the day your mother leaves this town. You'll be city marshal of Quicksand as long as she's here to know it. After I stir around town a bit and put 'em on I'll guarantee that nobody won't give the thing away to her. And say, you leather-headed, rip-roarin', low-down son of a locoed cyclone, you follow that advice she gave me! I'm going' to take some of it myself, too."

"Buck," said Calliope, feeling, "ef I don't I hope I may—"

"Shut up," said Buck. "She's a-comin back."

Cowboys Who Have Mothers, Too

Around the turn of the century, authors began to realize that more and more women were showing up on the frontier. And they began to predict, therefore, that the "wild and woolly West" was about to be tamed and curried.

Two stories come to mind. One is Stephen Crane's "The Bride Comes to Yellow Sky," published in 1898. In Crane's story Marshal Potter returns to town with his bride, and the first person they run into is a notorious troublemaker, Scratchy Wilson. He is drunk and looking for a shootout. But when Scratchy realizes that the marshal is actually *married*, he holsters his guns and sadly walks away. "Well," he says, "I s'pose it's all off now."

In O. Henry's "The Reformation of Calliope," it's the ruffian's mother who arrives to stop the shooting. There are several similarities between Crane's story and O. Henry's. In both plots, the gunslinger is drunk; he craves attention, preferably respect and terror; and he is challenged by resolute law officers who are going to shoot to kill. In "The Bride Comes to Yellow Sky" the marshal has already shot Scratchy, in a previous encounter, and would do it again if he had the chance.

The language of "The Reformation of Calliope" is a little hard to get used to, starting with the bully's nickname, which was given to him because he bellows like a steam organ (or "steam piano," as O. Henry says). The language makes this story sound like it is being told by a British butler; crossword puzzle addicts and Scrabble champions should love such vocabulary words as "wont" and "ennui" and "lugubrious."

But if we can overlook the stuffy rhetoric, there is an authentic flavor to this gunfight. Calliope is a misplaced southern redneck with a bad attitude, made worse by the fact that part of his job includes being nice to Easterners. When he drinks, his frustrations come to the surface. He is familiar with revolvers, and he shoots at dogs and minority citizens with equal pleasure. He is also pleased to have someone challenge him. In all respects he is a childish delinquent who has stepped over the line.

The ambush of Calliope seems realistic, too. A law officer who wanted to go on breathing was not likely to walk into the street and offer him a fair fight. It is more natural that the marshal and deputies would try to get rid of him in the most efficient—and safest—way possible. Therefore, the marshal's men shoot from cover and take no chances—until the train rolls up to the station and offers Calliope a chance to escape. At that point the marshal finally makes a rash move.

In "The Bride Comes to Yellow Sky," it is the marshal's wife who comes in on the train and brings about a peaceful change in the lawless shootist. Is the "reformation" of Calliope brought about by the marshal's mother arriving on the train? That's where O. Henry, famous for writing stories with surprise twists, decides to make this a gunfight tale with a unique outcome. Calliope changes in a most unexpected way.

Clarence E. Mulford

1883–1956

Who has never heard of Hopalong Cassidy? A few years ago it would have been hard to find an American who had not seen Hopalong—as played by William Boyd—in movies and on television. But that image, that white-haired, black-shirted figure of justice on the white horse, is a far cry from Mulford's original conception.

Mulford was born in Illinois, and his family moved to Brooklyn when he was a young boy. While growing up he was inspired by Owen Wister's *The Virginian*, and eventually he became a collector of western literature and trivia. From there it was a short step to trying his hand at writing westerns. After some success in the short story market, Mulford decided that he wanted to write a continuing saga to be told through a series of novels. Each novel in the series would feature the same cast of characters living out their adventures in the Southwest.

He got his chance in 1905 when *Outing* decided to let Mulford write his serialized westerns for their pages. Thus Hopalong Cassidy was born, in a travel magazine.

It would be more accurate to say that he was born as Bill Cassidy. The hard-drinking, rough-talking redhead got his nickname because of a limp, the result of a bullet wound in his thigh. Readers of the Hopalong books will remember other famous cowboys who came to life under Mulford's pen, with names like Johnny Nelson, Tex Ewalt, Red Connors, and Mesquite Jenkins.

In 1935 Mulford accepted an offer from Hollywood, where a series of films would be based on the Bar-20 saga, featuring Hopalong Cassidy as the central character. William Boyd got the part. His upright, sanitized version of Hopalong soon became a role model to young boys wherever there were movie theaters.

Mulford wrote a total of twenty-eight western novels. After his death in 1956, four more Hopalong Cassidy novels were written by Louis L'Amour under the pen name "Tex Burns." Two full-length films starred Hopalong, *The Deadwood Coach* and *Hopalong Cassidy*; shorter films, sixty-four of them altogether, were made for the double-feature matinee market between 1935 and 1948. The television series appeared between 1948 and 1952.

Hopalong Sits In

Hopalong Cassidy dismounted in front of the rough-boarded hotel, regarding it with a curious detachment which was the result of a lifetime's experience with such hybrid affairs. He knew what it would be even before he left the saddle: saloon, gambling house and hotel, to mention its characteristics in the order of their real importance.

Hopalong entered the main room and found that it ran the full length of the building. A bar paralleled one wall, card tables filled the open space; and in the inside corner near the door was a pine desk on which was a bottle of muddy ink, a corroded pen, a paper-covered notebook of the kind used in schools for compositions, and a grimy showcase holding cigars and tobaccos. Behind the desk on the wall was a short piece of board with nails driven in it, and on the nails hung a few keys.

A shiftless person with tobacco-stained lips arose from a near-by table, looking inquiringly at the newcomer.

"Got a room?" asked Hopalong.

"Yeah. Two dollars, in advance," replied the clerk.

"By the week," suggested Hopalong.

"Twelve dollars—we don't count Sundays," said the clerk with a foolish grin.

"Eat on the premises?" asked the newcomer, sliding a gold coin across the desk.

The clerk tossed the coin into the air, listened to the ring as it struck the board, tossed it into a drawer, made change and hooked a thumb over his shoulder.

"Right in yonder," he said, indicating the other half of the building. "Doors open six to eight; twelve to one; six to seven. Pay when you eat an' take what you get. Come with me an' I'll show you the room."

Hopalong obeyed, climbing the steep and economical stairs with just the faintest suggestion of a limp. As they passed down the central hall, he could see into the rooms on each side. They were all alike, even to the arrangement of the furniture. The beds all stood with their heads against the hall wall, in the same relative positions.

"Reckon this will do," he grunted, looking past the clerk into the room indicated. "Stable out back?"

"Yeah. Take yore hoss around an' talk to the stableman," said the clerk, facing around. "Dinner in about an hour."

Hopalong nodded and fell in behind his guide, found the stairs worse in descent than in ascent, and arranged for the care of his horse. When he returned to the room he dropped his blanket roll on the foot of the bed, and then looked searchingly and slowly at the canvas walls. There was nothing to be seen, and shaking his head gently, he went out and down again to wander about the town until time to enter the dining room.

After dinner he saddled his horse and rode down the wide cattle trail, going southward in hope of meeting the sv herd. This was the day it was due; but he was too old a hand to worry about a trail herd being behind time. Johnny Nelson would reach the town when he got there, and there was no reason to waste any thought about the matter. Still, he had nothing else to do, and he pushed on at an easy lope.

He, himself, had been over at Dodge City, where he had learned that Johnny Nelson had a herd on the trail and was bound north. It was a small herd of selected cattle driven by a small outfit. He had not seen Johnny for over a year, and it was too good an opportunity to let pass. For the pleasure of meeting his old friend he had written a letter to him addressed to an important mail station on the new trail, where all outfits called for mail. Some days later he had left Dodge and ridden west, and now he was on hand to welcome the sv owner.

Hopalong passed two herds as he rode, and paused to exchange words with the trail bosses. One of the herds was bound for Wyoming, and the other for Dakota. Trailing had not been very brisk so far this season, but from what the two bosses had heard it was due to pick up shortly. About mid-afternoon Hopalong turned and started back toward town, reaching the hotel soon after the dining-room doors opened.

After supper the town came to life, and as darkness fell, the street was pretty well filled with men. The greater part of the town's population was floating: punchers, gamblers and others whose occupations were not so well known.

The main room of the hotel came to life swiftly, the long bar was well lined and the small tables began to fill. The noise increased in volume and it was not long before the place was in full swing. From time to time brawls broke out in the street and made themselves heard; and once pistol shots caused heads to raise and partly stilled the room.

Hopalong sat lazily in a chair between two windows, his back to the wall, placidly engaged in watching the activities about him. More and more his eyes turned to one particular table, where a game of poker was under way, and where the rounds of drinks came in a steady procession. His curiosity was aroused, and he wondered if the situation was the old one.

To find out, he watched to see which player drank the least liquor, and he found that instead of one man doing that, there were two. To a man of Hopalong's experience along the old frontier, that suggested a very pertinent thought; and he watched more keenly now to see if he could justify it. So far as he was concerned, it was purely an impersonal matter; he knew none of the players and cared nothing who lost in the game. As hand followed hand, and the liquor began to work, the cheating became apparent to him and threatened to become apparent to others; and he found his gorge slowly rising.

Finally one of the players, having lost his last chip and being unable to buy more, pushed back his chair and left the table, reeling toward the street door. Just then, elbowing his way from the crowd at the bar, came one of the trail bosses with whom Hopalong had talked that afternoon. The newcomer stopped behind the vacant chair and gestured toward it inquiringly.

"Shore. Set down," said one of the sober players. The others nodded their acquiescence, soberly or drunkenly as the case might be, and more drinks were ordered. The two sober men had drunk round for round with the others, and yet showed no effects from it. Hopalong flashed a glance at the bar, and nodded wisely. Very likely they were being served tea.

Hopalong pulled his chair out from the wall, tipped it back and settled down, his big hat slanting well before his eyes. He had ridden all day and was tired, and he found himself drowsing. After an interval, the length of which he did not know, he was aroused to alertness by a shouted curse; but before he could get to his feet or roll off the chair, a shot roared out, almost deafening him. There was a quick flurry at the table, a struggle, and he saw the trail boss, disarmed, being dragged and pushed toward the door. Hopalong removed his sombrero and looked at the hole near the edge of the brim. He was inserting the tip of his little finger into it when one of the players, in a hurried glance around the room, saw the action.

"Close, huh?" inquired the gambler with momentary interest, and then looked around the room again. Several men had pushed out from the crowd and stood waiting in a little group, closely watching the room. As he glimpsed these men, the gambler's face lost its trace of anxiety and he smiled coldly.

Hopalong's eyes flicked from the gambler to the watchful guards and back again, and then he turned slowly to look at the wall behind him, just back of his right ear. The bullet hole was there.

"Yeah, it was close," he said slowly, grinning grimly. "At first I reckoned mebby it might be an old one; but that hole in the wall says it ain't. Who stepped on that fool's pet corn?"

"Nobody; just too much liquor," answered the gambler. "Sometimes it makes a man ugly. Now he's busted up the game, for I shore don't care for a four-hander. Mebby you'd like to take his place?"

"I might," admitted Hopalong with no especial interest. "What you playin', an' how steep?"

"Draw, with jackpots after a full house or better," replied the gambler, looking swiftly but appraisingly at the two drunken players. They had leaned over the table again, and were not to be counted upon to make denials of any statement. "Two bits, an' two dollars; just a friendly game, to pass away the time."

"All right," replied Hopalong, thinking that friendship came rather high in Trailville, if that was the measure of a friendly game.

The gambler waved a hand, and four men stepped to the table. After a moment's argument they took the helpless players from their chairs and started them toward the front door.

Hopalong smiled, thinking that now the game was less than four-handed. He said nothing, however, but stepped forward and dropped into one of the vacant chairs.

"We can get a couple more to take their places," Hopalong said, and nodded gently as his prophecy was fulfilled. He smiled a welcome to the two men and waited until the gambler had taken his own chair. Then Hopalong leaned forward. "You can call me Riordan," he said.

"Kitty out a white chip every game for the house," said the gambler, reaching for the cards. "We play straights between threes and flushes; no fancy combinations. A faced card on the draw can't be taken."

"You playin' for the house?" asked Hopalong needlessly. He was drawing a hand from a pocket as he spoke, and at the gambler's answering nod, he opened the hand and pushed the coins toward the other. "You got chips enough to sell me some," he said.

The game got under way, and the liquor began to arrive. Hopalong was smiling inwardly: he was well fortified to meet the conditions of this game. In the first place, he could stand an amazing amount of whisky; but he did not intend to crowd his capacity by drinking every round. In the second, poker was to him a fine art; and the more dishonest the game, the finer his art—thanks to Tex Ewalt. He always met crookedness with crookedness rather than to cause trouble, but he let the others set the pace.

He looked like a common frontier citizen, with perhaps a month's wages in his pockets, and he believed that was the reason for the moderate limit set by the gambler, who was a tinhorn, and satisfied with small pickings if he could not do better; but as a matter of fact, Hopalong was a full partner in a very prosperous northern ranch, and he could write a check for six figures and have it honored. Last, and fully as important, he was able to take care of himself in any frontier situation from cutting cards to shooting lead. He believed that he was going to thoroughly enjoy his stay in Trailville.

"On the trail?" carelessly asked the gambler as the cards were cut for the first deal.

"No," answered Hopalong, picking up the deck by diagonal corners in case the cards had been shaved. "I'm just driftin' toward home."

As the game went on it appeared that he had a bad poker weakness: every time he had a poor hand and bluffed strongly, his mouth twitched. It took some time for this to register with the others, but when it did, he found that he was very promptly called; and his displeasure in his adversaries' second sight was plain to all who watched.

Along about the middle of the game his mouth must have twitched by accident, for he raked in a pot that had been well built up and leveled up nearly all his loss. The game seesawed until midnight, when it broke up; and Hopalong found that he cashed in twenty dollars less chips than he had bought; twenty dollars' worth of seeds, from which a crop might grow. He knew that he would be a welcomed addition to any poker game in this hotel, that his weaknesses were known, and his consistent and set playing was now no secret.

He went to his room, closed the door and lighted the lamp, intending to go to bed; but the room was too hot for comfort. There was not a breath of air stirring, and as yet the coolness of the night had not overcome the heat stored up by the walls and roof during the day. He stood for a moment in indecision and then, knowing that another hour would make an appreciable difference in the temperature of the room, he turned and left it, going down to the street.

The night was dark, but star-bright, and he stood for a moment looking about him. The saloons and gambling shacks were going full blast, but they had no appeal for him. He walked toward the corner of the hotel and looked back toward the stables; and then he remembered that he had seen a box against the side wall of the bar-room. That was just what he wanted, and he moved slowly along the wall, feeling his way in the deeper shadow, found it, and seated himself with a sigh of relief, leaning back against the wall and relaxing.

Men passed up and down the street, and human voices rose and fell in the buildings along it. Time passed with no attempt on Hopalong's part to keep track of it, but by the deepening chill which comes at that altitude, he believed that the room would now be bearable. About to get up and make a start for the street, he heard and saw two men lazily approach the corner of the building and lean against it, and glance swiftly about them. From the faint light of the front window he thought that he knew who one of them was; and as soon as the man spoke, he was certain of the identity.

"You know what to do," said the speaker. "I looked 'em over good. There's about two hundred head of fine, selected cattle, four-year-olds. It'll be easy to run off most of 'em, or mebby all of 'em. Take 'em round about into Wolf Hollow, an' then scatter 'em to hell an' gone. We'll round 'em up later. Don't bungle it *this* time. Get goin'."

The two men separated, one moving swiftly to where a horse was standing across the street. He mounted quickly and rode away. The other moved out of sight around the corner and disappeared, apparently into the hotel. Three men came past the corner and paused to argue drunkenly; and by the time they had moved on again Hopalong knew that he had lost touch with the man who held his interest.

The coast being clear, Hopalong moved slowly toward the street, went into the bar-room and glanced about as he made his way to the stairs. Reaching his room, he closed the door behind him and listened for a few minutes. During lulls in the general noise downstairs he could hear a man snoring.

Undressing, he stretched out and gave himself over to a period of quiet but intensive thought. He had nothing positive to go upon; the horseman had ridden off so quickly that he was gone before Hopalong could come to any decision about following him; he realized that by the time he could have saddled up the man would have been out of reach. He did not know for sure that the two men had referred to the sv herd, nor where to find it if he did know. All he could do was to wait, and to keep his ears open and his wits about him. It would be better to conceal his interest in Johnny Nelson and Johnny's cattle. As a matter of fact he had nothing but unfounded suspicions for the whole structure he was building up.

Back in Dodge City he had been well informed about Trailville and the conditions obtaining there, since a large per cent of the unholy population of Dodge had packed up and gone to the new town. The big herds no longer crossed the Arkansas near the famous old cattle town, to amble up the divide leading to the Sawlog. The present marshal of Dodge was a good friend of Hopalong's, and had been thorough in his pointers and remarks.

Hopalong had learned from him, for one thing, that a good trail herd with a small outfit would be likely to lose cattle and have a deal of trouble before it passed the new town; especially if the trail crew was further reduced in numbers by some of the men receiving time off to enjoy an evening in the town. Further than that the marshal had mentioned one man by name, Bradley, and stressed it emphatically; and only tonight Hopalong had heard that man's name called out while the poker game was under way, and had looked with assumed carelessness across the table at the player who had answered to it.

Hopalong had taken pains during the remainder of the evening to be affable to this gentleman, and to study him; he had been so affable and friendly that he even had forborne giving a hint that he knew the gentleman cheated when occasion seemed to warrant it. And this man Bradley was the man he had overheard speak just a few minutes before at the corner of the building.

Perhaps, after all, he would ride down the trail in the morning, if he knew that he was not observed doing it, and try to get in touch with Johnny, even though he did not know how far away the sv herd might be. He knew that the herd numbered about two hundred head of the best cattle to be found on four ranches; and he knew that the outfit would be small. He feared . . . Ah, hell! What was the use of letting unfounded suspicions make a fool of him, and keep him awake? He turned over on his side and went to sleep like a child.

He was the second man through the dining-room door the next morning, and soon thereafter he left town, bound down the trail, hoping that the sv herd was within a day's ride, and that he could meet it unobserved. He had not covered a dozen miles before he saw a horseman coming toward him up the trail, and something about the man seemed familiar. It was not long before he knew the rider to be Bradley.

The two horsemen nodded casually and pulled up, stopping almost leg to leg.

"Leavin' us, Riordan?" asked the upbound man.

"No," answered Hopalong. "The town's dead durin' daylight, an' I figgered to look over the country an' kill some time."

"There ain't nothin' down this way to see," replied the other. "Nor up the other way, neither," he added.

"Ride with you, then, as far as town," said Hopalong, deciding not to show even a single card of his hand.

They went on up the trail at a slow and easy gait, talking idly of this and that, and then Hopalong turned sidewise and asked a question with elaborate casualness.

"Who's town marshal, Bradley?" he asked.

"Slick Cunningham. Why?" asked Bradley, flashing a quick glance at his companion.

Hopalong was silent for a moment, turning the name over in his mind; and then his expression faintly suggested relief.

"Never heard of him," he admitted, and laughed gently, his careless good nature once more restored. "Reckon, accordin' to that, he never heard of me, neither."

"Oh, Slick's all right; he minds his own business purty well," said Bradley, and grinned broadly. "Anyhow, he's out of town right now."

Continuing a purely idle conversation, they soon saw the town off on one side of the trail, and Bradley raised a hand.

"There she is," he said, pulling up. "I've got a couple of errands to do that wouldn't interest you none; so I'll quit you here, an' see you in town tonight."

"Keno," grunted Hopalong, and headed for the collection of shacks that was Trailville. He was halfway to town when he purposely lost his hat. Wheeling, he swung down to scoop it up, and took advantage of the movement to glance swiftly backward; and he was just in time to see Bradley dipping down into a hollow west of the trail. The remainder of the short ride was covered at a walk, and was a thoughtful one.

The day dragged past, suppertime came and went, and again the big room slowly filled with men. Hopalong sat in the same chair, tipped back against the wall, the bullet hole close to his head. Bradley soon came in, stopping at the bar for a few moments, and then led the same group of card players to the same table. Looking around for Hopalong, they espied him, called him by his name of Riordan and gestured toward the table. In a few moments the game was under way.

The crowd shifted constantly, men coming and going from and to the street. There was a group bunched at the bar, close to the front door. Two men came in from the street, pushing along the far side of the group, eager to quench their thirst. One of them was Slick Cunningham, town marshal, just back from a special assignment. His name was not even as old as Trail-ville. He glanced through a small opening in the group to see who was in the room, and as his gaze settled on the men playing cards with Bradley, he stiff-ened and stepped quickly backward, covered by the group.

"Outside, George," he whispered to his companion. "Pronto! Stand just outside the door an' wait for me!"

George was mildly surprised, but he turned and sauntered to the street, stopping when he reached it.

The marshal was nowhere in sight, but he soon appeared around the cor-ner of the building, and beckoned his friend to his side.

"I just had a good look through the window," he said hurriedly. "I knowed it was him; an' it shore is! When Bradley said he was figgerin' on takin' his pick of that sv herd I told him, an' all of you, too, that he was get-tin' ready to pull a grizzly's tail. An' he is! Nelson was one of the old Bar 20 gang. . . . An' who the hell do you reckon is sittin' between Bradley an' Winters, playin' poker with 'em? Hopalong Cassidy! Hopalong Cassidy, damn his soul!"

"Thought you said he was up in Montanny?" replied George, with only casual interest.

"He was! But, great Gawd! he don't have to stay there, does he? You get word to Bradley, quick as you can. Settin' elbow to elbow with Cassidy! If that don't stink, then I don't know what does! Cassidy here in Trailville, an' Nelson's cattle comin' up the trail! I'm tellin' you that somethin's wrong!"

"You reckon he knows anything?" asked George, to whom the name of Hopalong Cassidy did not mean nearly so much as it did to his companion.

"Listen!" retorted the marshal earnestly. "Nobody on Gawd's gray earth knows how much that feller knows! I've never run up ag'in him yet when he didn't know a damn sight more than I wanted him to; an' what he don't know, he damn soon finds out. You get word to Bradley. I'm pullin' out of town, an' I'm stayin' out till this mess is all cleaned up. If Cassidy sees me, he'll know that I know him, he'll know that I'll pass on the word to my friends. I'll give a hundred dollars to see him buried."

"You mean that?" asked George, with sudden interest.

Slick peered into his eyes through the gloom, and then snorted with disgust.

"Don't you be a damn fool!" he snapped. "I didn't say that I wanted to see *you* buried, did I?"

"Hell with that!" retorted George. "I'm askin' you if you really mean that as an offer; if you'll pay a hundred dollars to the man that kills him?"

"Well, I didn't reckon nobody would be fool enough to take me up," said Slick, but he suddenly leaned forward again, as a new phase of the matter struck him. "Yes, you damn fool! Yes, I will!" He pulled his hat down firmly and nodded. "My share of that herd money will come to a lot more than a hundred dollars; but if that pizen pup stays alive around here we won't steal a head, an' I won't get a cent. Yes, the offer goes; but you better get help, an' split it three ways. There's only one man in town who would have any kind of a chance, an' his name ain't George."

"I'll take care of that end of it," replied George; "an' now I'm goin' in to get word to Bradley. So long."

"So long," said Slick, and forthwith disappeared around the corner on his way to the little corral behind the marshal's office. There was a good horse in that corral, and a horse was just what he wanted at the moment.

George pushed through the group, signaled to the bartender, ordered a drink, and whispered across the counter. Placing his glass on the bar, George moved carelessly down the room, nodding to right and to left. He stopped beside the busy poker table, grunted a greeting to the men he knew, and dragged up a chair near Bradley's right elbow, where he could look at the cards in his friend's hand, and by merely raising his eyes, looked over their tops at the player on the left.

Hopalong had dropped out for that deal, and was leaning back in his chair, his eyes shaded by the brim of his hat. His placid gaze was fixed on the window opposite and he was wondering whose face it was that he had glimpsed in the little patch of light outside. The face had been well back, and the beams of light from the lamps had not revealed it well; but it was something to think about, and, having nothing else to do at the moment, he let his mind dwell on it. He did not like faces furtively peering in through lighted windows.

Bradley chuckled, pulled in the pot and tossed his cards unshown into the discard.

"Hello, George," he said, turning to smile at the man on his right.

"Hello, Bill. Won't nobody call yore hand tonight?"

"They don't call me at the right time," laughed Bradley, in rare good humor. "This seems to be my night." He looked up at the man who now stepped into his circle of vision. "What is it, Tom?"

"Bartender wants to see you, Bill. Says it's important, an' won't take more'n a minute."

"Deal me out this hand," said Bradley, pushing back his chair and following the messenger.

Hopalong let the cards lay as they fell, and when the fifth had dropped in front of him his fingers pushed them into a neat, smooth-sided book, and he watched the faces of the other players as the hands were picked up. The house gambler was in direct line with that part of the bar where Bradley had stopped, and Hopalong's gaze, lifting from the face of the player, for a moment picked out Bradley and the bartender. The latter was looking straight at him and the expression on the man's face was grim and hostile. Hopalong looked at the next player, lifted his own cards and riffled the corners to let the pips flash before his eyes.

"She's open," said the man on the dealer's left, tossing a chip into the center of the table.

"Stay," grunted Hopalong, doing likewise in his turn. A furtive face at the window, a message for Bradley, and a suddenly hostile bartender—and Johnny's herd was small, selected, and had a small outfit with it. Suspicions, suspicions, always suspicions! He bent his head, and then raised it quickly and looked at George before that person had time to iron out his countenance. From that instant Hopalong did not like George, and determined to keep an eye on him.

Bradley returned, slapped George on the shoulder and drew up to the table, watching the play. Not once did he look at Hopalong.

When the play came around to Hopalong it had been raised twice, and that person, studying his cards intently, suddenly looked over their tops and tossed them away. Bradley's expression changed a flash too late.

"They ain't runnin' for me," growled Hopalong, glancing from Bradley to George. "Game's gettin' tiresome, but I'll try a few more hands."

"Hell!" growled Bradley, affable and smiling again. "That ain't the trouble—the game's too small to hold a feller's interest."

"Right!" quickly said the house gambler, nodding emphatically as he sensed a kill. "Too tee-totally damn small! Let's play a round of jackpots to finish this up; an' then them that don't want to play for real money can't say they was throwed out cold."

"I'll set out the round of jacks an' come in on the new game," said Hopalong, risking quick glances around the room. No one seemed to be paying any particular attention to him.

"Me, too. No, I'll give you fellers a chance," said Bradley.

"Don't need to give me no chance," said a player across from him. "I'm ready for the big game."

Hopalong saw a young man push through the crowd near the door and head straight for the table. As he made his way down the room he was the cynosure of all eyes, and a ripple of whispered comment followed him. Hopalong did not know it, but the newcomer was a killer famous for his deeds around Trailville—a man who would kill for money, who had always "got" his man, and who was a close friend of Bradley's.

"Hello, Bill," the newcomer addressed Bradley, and then dropped into the chair which George surrendered to him as if he was expected to do so; and thereupon George moved toward the bar and was lost to sight.

Bradley nodded, smiled and faced the table again, gesturing with both hands.

"Riordan, meet Jim Hawes. Jim, Riordan's a stranger here."

The two men exchanged nods, sizing each other up. Hawes saw a typical cowpuncher, past middle age; but a man whose deeds rang from one edge of the cattle country to the other; a man whose reputation would greatly enhance that of anybody who managed to kill him with a gun in an even break. His mantle of fame would rest automatically upon the shoulders of his master.

Hopalong saw a vicious-faced killer, cold, unemotional, and of almost tender years. There was a swagger in his every movement and one could easily see that he was an important individual. The young man's eyes were rather close together, and his chin receded. To Hopalong, both of these characteristics were danger marks. He had found, in his own experience, that the prognathous jaw is greatly overrated. Hawes reminded him of a weasel.

"Haven't had a game for a long time," said Hawes, speaking with almost pugnacious assurance. "Reckon I'll set in an' give her a whirl."

"She's goin' to be a real one, Jim," said the house dealer uneasily. His profession, to his way of thinking, called for a little trickery with the cards upon occasion; but with Jim Hawes in the game only an adept would dare attempt it; not so much that Hawes was capable of detecting fine work, but because he would shoot with as little compunction as a rattler strikes.

"I like 'em big; the bigger the better," boasted Hawes, his cold eyes on Hopalong. "What you say, Riordan?" he asked, and the way he said the words made them a challenge. It appeared that his humor was not a pleasant one tonight.

"I'd rather have 'em growed up," replied Hopalong, looking him in the eyes, "*Well* growed up," amended Hopalong, his gaze unswerving.

Somewhere in the room a snicker sounded, quickly hushed as Hawes glanced toward the sound. The room had grown considerably quieter, ears functioning instead of tongues, and this, in itself, was a hint to an observing man. Hawes' gaze was back again like a flash, and he kept it set on the stranger's face while he slowly, with his left hand, drew his chair closer to the table, in the space provided for him by Bradley. He, too, sensed the quiet of the room, and a tight, knowing smile wreathed his thin lips.

"We'll make it growed up enough for you, Mister Riordan," he said, his left hand now drawing a roll of bills from a pocket. "How's five, an' twenty?" he challenged.

"Cents or dollars," curiously asked Hopalong, his face expressionless.

Hawes flushed, but checked the fighting words before they reached his teeth.

"What makes *you* reckon it might be cents?" he demanded, triumphantly.

"Just had a feelin' that it might be," calmly answered Hopalong. "Either one is a waste of time."

Bradley raised his eyebrows, regarding the speaker intently.

"Yeah?" he softly inquired. "How do you grade a growed-up game?"

"It all depends who I'm playin' with," answered Hopalong, his eyes on Hawes' tense face.

"Five an' fifty—*dollars!*" snapped the youth, showing his teeth.

"She's improvin' with every word," chuckled the house player.

"Damn near of age, anyhow," said Hopalong, nodding. "Straight draw poker? Threes, straights, flushes, an' so forth? No fancy hands?"

"The same game we have been playin'," said the house player. "Jackpots after full houses, or better. That suit everybody?"

Silence gave consent, the chips were redeemed at the old figure, deftly stacked and counted by the house player, and resold at the new prices. Hopalong drew out a roll of dirty bills, peeled off two of them, and with them bought a thousand dollars' worth of chips. He placed the remainder of the roll on the table near the chips, and nodded at it.

"When that's gone, I'm busted," he said, and looked at Hawes.

"Oh, don't worry! There's mine," sneered the youth, and bought the same amount of counters. Inwardly he thrilled; in so steep a game, cheating would be a great temptation to anyone inclined that way; and a crooked play would be justification for what followed it, and would suit him as well as any other excuse.

The player who had announced that he was ready for the bigger game now raised both hands toward heaven, pushed back his chair, and motioned grandiloquently toward the table; but no one in the room cared to take his place: the game was far too steep for them, and they sensed a deadly atmosphere.

"Quittin' us Frank?" asked Bradley, with a knowing grin.

"Cold an' positive! My money comes harder than your'n, Bradley; an' I ain't got near as much of it. No, sir! I'll get all the excitement I'll need, just settin' back an' watchin' the play."

He had been sitting on Hopalong's left, and when he withdrew from the game, he pulled his chair back from the table, and now he drew it farther out of the way. Hopalong shifted in that direction, to even up the spacing; but as he stopped, he sensed Bradley's nearness, and saw that the latter had moved after him, but too far. Bradley's impetus had carried him even closer to Hopalong than he had been before. Bradley smiled apologetically and moved back, but only for a few inches. The fleeting expression on Hawes' face revealed satisfaction, and dressed the blundering shift with intent. What intent? In Hopalong's mind there could be only one; and that one, deadly.

The game got under way, and it was different from the more or less innocent affair which had preceded it. It was different in more ways than one. In the first place there was now present a thinly veiled hostility, an atmosphere of danger. In the second, a man could bluff with more assurance; a player would think twice before he would toss in fifty dollars to call a hand when he, himself, held little. In the third, a clever card manipulator would be tempted to make use of his best mastered tricks of sleight of hand; and should any man call for a new deck, or palm the old one for a moment, it would be well to give thought to the possible substitution of a cold deck. Here was the kind of a game Hopalong could enjoy; he had cut his teeth on them, and had been given excellent instruction by a past master of the game. Tex Ewalt had pronounced him proficient.

The first few hands were more in the nature of skirmishes, for with the change in the stakes had come a change in the style of play. Hopalong's fingers were calloused, but the backs of his fingers were not; and he now bunched his cards in his left hand, face to the palm, and let the backs of the fingers of his right hand brush gently down the involved patterns, searching for pin pricks. As the cards were dealt to him, Hopalong idly pushed them about on the table, to get a different slant of lamplight on each one. If the polish had been removed by abrasives or acids the reflected light would show it.

At last came a jackpot, and it was passed three times, growing greatly in the process. The house player picked up the cards to deal, shuffling them swiftly, and ruffled them together with both hands hiding them. He pushed the deck toward Hopalong for the cut, in such a manner that if the latter chose the easier and more natural movement, he would cut with his nearest, or left, hand. If he did this, his fingers would naturally grasp the sides of the deck, and not the ends; and if the cards were trimmed, such a cut might well be costly.

As the dealer took his hand off the deck, Hopalong let his left hand reach for his cigarette; and it being thus occupied, and quite innocently so, he reached across his body with the idle right and quite naturally picked up the upper part of the deck by the ends. The dealer showed just the slightest indication of annoyance at this loss of time, and, finding Hopalong's bland gaze on the cards, forewent switching the cut, and dealt them as they lay.

Hawes opened for ten dollars. Bradley saw and raised it only five. Hopalong qualified. The dealer saw, and Hawes saw Bradley's raise, and boosted the limit. The others dropped out. Hawes showed his openers and took the pot. As the play went on, Hopalong observed a strange coincidence. The ante was five dollars; the limit, fifty. Every time that Hawes opened for ten dollars, and Bradley raised it five, or Bradley opened for ten, and Hawes raised it five, the opener thereupon boosted the limit when his time came, and very often dropped out on the next round to let the other win. Here was team work: Hawes and Bradley vs. all.

Hopalong glanced inquiringly at the house player, and caught an almost imperceptible wink directed at himself. There was no need for these two men to go into conference where teamwork was concerned; they knew how to join forces without previous agreements. And now, teamwork was called for as a matter of self-preservation.

The play went on without much action, and Hawes picked up the cards, bunching them for the deal. He was not an expert, and a dozen men in the room saw the clumsy switch, and held their breaths; but nothing violent happened. Apparently the other three players had not seen anything of interest. Bradley opened for ten dollars. Hopalong, looking at his cards, saw three kings and a pair of tens. He passed, and smiled inwardly at the dealer's poorly concealed look of amazement. The house player saw, but when both Hawes and Bradley had raised the limit in turn, he threw his hand in the discard and watched Bradley take the pot by default.

Hopalong, toying idly with his cards, now looked at them again, and swore loudly and bitterly.

"Damn fool! I thought it was two pairs . . . Will you *look* at *that?*"

Hopalong's outspread cards revealed their true worth, and the house player chuckled deep in his throat, his eyes beaming with congratulations.

"Pat king full," he said. "Well, Riordan, it can be beat."

"It can," admitted Hopalong, trying to smile. For an instant the two men looked understandingly into each other's eyes.

There was now no question about the status of this game. Both Hopalong and the house player had seen the clumsy switch; and it had been followed by a pat king full. The bars were now down and the rules were up. It was just a case of outcheating cheaters, and the devil takes the less adept.

On Bradley's deal Hawes took another small pot by default, and Hopalong picked up the cards. His big hands moved swiftly, his fingers flicking almost in a blur of speed. The house player watched him, and then, curiously, against his habit, picked up each card as it fell in front of him. Seven, five, eight, and six of hearts. The fifth card seemed to intrigue him greatly: with it he would get the measure of a dexterous player's real mentality; and he hoped desperately that he would not have to play a pat hand. He sighed, picked up the card, and saw the jack of clubs. For a moment he regarded the dealer thoughtfully, and almost affectionately, and then he swiftly made up his mind. He would risk one play for the sake of knowledge. He opened for a white chip.

Hawes saw, and raised a red. Bradley stayed. Hopalong dropped out. The house player saw, and raised a blue, a true mark of confidence in a stranger's dealing ability; and almost before the chips had struck the table, Hawes saw and raised the limit. Bradley stayed, and the house player, rubbing his chin thoughtfully, evened it up, and asked for one card. He looked at it and turned it over, face up on the table. It was the four of hearts.

"Thanks," he said, nodding to Hopalong. "I needed that. It costs fifty dollars to play with me," he said to the others.

Hawes thought swiftly. As a heart, the card would fill a flush; as a four spot, it would built up three of a kind, a straight, a full house or four of a kind. Had it been a jack he would have hesitated; but now he tried to hide his elation, and tossed in a hundred dollars to see and to raise. Bradley sighed and dropped out.

"You took two cards," murmured the house player thoughtfully. "Mebby—mebby you got another; but I doubt it. She's up ag'in."

"Once more," said Hawes, his eyes glinting.

"Well, it's my business to know a bluff when I see one," said the house player, studying his adversary. "It's my best judgment that you . . . Well, anyhow, I'll back it, Hawes, an' boost her once more."

"*Gracias!*" laughed Hawes, a little tensely. "When I went to school a four spot was a right small card. See you, an' raise ag'in."

"An' once more."

"Ag'in."

"Once more."

"Ag'in."

"An' once more," said the house player. "I allus like to play a hand like this clean to the end. They're right scarce."

Suddenly Hawes had a disturbing suspicion. Could it be that this opponent had held four of a kind pat? He, himself, had thrown away an ace and a queen. That left two possible high fours: kings or jacks. He looked at his own cards, and decided that he had pressed them for all they were worth.

"Then show it to me!" he growled, calling.

"It's the gambler's prayer," said the house player, laying down his cards slowly and one by one. The five of hearts joined the face-up four; then the six, and then the seven. He looked calmly over the top of the last card, holding it close to his face; and then, sighing, placed it where it belonged, and dropped both hands under the edge of the table.

"Straight flush," he said calmly.

Hawes flushed and then went pale. Both of his hands were on the table, while the house player's were out of sight. He swore in his throat and started to toss his cards into the discard, but the house player checked him.

"It's a showdown, Hawes. I paid as much to see your hand as you paid to see mine. Turn 'em over."

Hawes obeyed, slamming the cards viciously, and four pleasant ten-spots lay in orderly array.

"Hard luck for a man to get a hand like that at the wrong time," said the winner.

He drew in the chips and picked up the cards. A thought passed through his mind: when playing with keen, smart men, a foolish play will often win. In such a case, two successive bluffs often pay dividends. The house player chuckled in his throat.

"Jacks to open this one," the house player—it was his deal—announced as Hopalong cut. It pleased him to see the way in which Hopalong followed the natural way to cut the deck, and lifted it by the sides; but it only showed confidence, because the dealer wanted no cut at all, and switched it perfectly as he took it up again. In what he was about to do, he would accomplish two things: he would return a favor, and also help Hawes into the situation the latter had been looking for. To make plain his own innocence in the matter, he talked while he dealt.

"The art of cuttin' cards is a fine one," he said. "You hear a lot about slick dealin', but hardly a word about slick cuttin'. That's because it's mighty rare. Why, once I knowed a feller that could cut . . . Oh, well. I'll tell the story after the hand is played."

But it so happened that the house player never told that lie.

Hawes passed. Bradley opened for ten. Hopalong stayed, and the dealer dropped out. Hawes raised it five, and Bradley tossed in a blue and a white chip, seeing, and raising the limit. Hopalong leveled up and added another blue. Hawes dropped out. Bradley studied his hand and saw. He drew two cards and Hopalong took one. The latter would have been very much surprised if he had been disappointed, for he had detected the switched cut. Bradley pushed out a blue chip, and Hopalong saw and raised another. Bradley pushed in two, and Hopalong two more. Back and forth it went, time after time.

Hawes leaned over and looked at Bradley's hand. He studied Hopalong a moment, and gave thought to the straight flush he had just had the misfortune to call. Straight flushes do not come two in a row—at least, that was so in his experience. He leaned forward, his left hand resting on his piled chips.

"Side bet, Riordan?" he inquired sneeringly.

"How much?" asked Hopalong, a little nervously.

"How much you got?" snapped Hawes.

"Plenty."

"Huh! Dollars, or *cents*?" sneered Hawes, quoting an unpleasant phrase.

"Dollars. Lemme see. Five, ten, fifteen, twenty, twenty-five, thirty, thirty-five, forty, forty-one, two, three, four, five, six—forty-six hundred, leavin' me ham an' aig money. You scared?"

"Scared hell!" snapped Hawes. He counted his own resources, found them greatly short, and looked inquiringly at Bradley. "Lend me the difference?" he asked.

Bradley nodded, and beckoned to the head bartender.

"Give Hawes what he needs, an' put a memo in the safe," he ordered.

In a few moments the game went on, the side bets lying apart from the pot. Then Bradley, grinning triumphantly, raised the limit again, certain that Riordan did not have money enough left to meet it. It was a sucker trick, but sometimes it worked.

Hopalong looked at him curiously, hesitated, went through his pockets, and then turned a worried face to his adversary.

"Anybody in the room lend me fifty dollars?" he asked, loudly; and not a voice replied. Hawes' malignant gaze had swept the crowd and held it silent. Not a man dared to comply with the request.

"Is that the way you win yore pots, Bradley? asked Hopalong coldly.

"I've raised you. Call or quit."

Hopalong's right hand dug down into a pocket, and he laughed nastily as he dropped a fifty-dollar bill on top of the chips in the center of the table.

"What you got, tin-horn?" he asked.

"I got the gambler's second prayer," chuckled Bradley, exposing four aces, and reaching for the pot.

"But I got the first," grunted Hopalong. "Same little run of hearts that we saw before."

For a moment there was an utter silence, and then came a blur of speed from Hawes, but just the instant before it came, Bradley fell off his chair to the left, his own left arm falling across Hopalong's right forearm, blocking a draw; but other men had discovered, when too late, that Hopalong's left hand was the better of the two. The double roar seemed to bend the walls, and sent the lamp flames leaping, to flicker almost to extinction. One went out, the other two recovered. The smoke thinned to show Hawes sliding from his chair, and Bradley on the floor where he had fallen by his own choice, with both hands straining at the Mexican spur which spiked his cheek.

The two leveled Colts held the crowd frozen in curious postures. Hands were raised high, or held out well away from belts. Hopalong backed to the wall, his left-hand gun still smoking. He felt the wall press against him, and then he nodded swiftly to the house player.

"You had a hell of a lot to say about the cut, after you switched it! Now, let's see what you know about a *draw*!" As Hopalong spoke, he shoved both guns into their sheaths, and slowly crossed his arms.

The gambler made no move, scarcely daring to breathe. He still doubted his senses.

"All right, then. Get out, an' stay out!" ordered Hopalong, and as the house player passed through the door, another man came in; a man unsteady on his feet, and covered with sweat and dust and blood.

The newcomer leaned against the bar for a moment, his gaze searching the room; and as he saw his old friend, Hopalong Cassidy, his old friend recognized him. It was Johnny Nelson.

"Hoppy!" he called, joyously.

"Johnny! What's up?"

"They rushed us in the dark, an' shot all of us up. Not seriously, but we're out of action. They got every head—near two hundred!"

Johnny Nelson's gaze wavered, rested for an instant on the open window to one side of his friend, and across the room from him; and, vague and unsteady as he was, he yielded to the gunman's instinct. His right hand dropped, and twisted up like a flash to the top of the holster, and the crash of his shot became a scream in the night outside the open window. George had lost his hundred-dollar fee—and with it, his life.

"Pullin' down on you, from the dark, Hoppy; but I got the skunk," muttered Johnny. He leaned against the bar again and took the whisky which an ingratiating bartender placed under his nose. "They got 'em all, Hoppy— near two hundred head."

Hopalong had his back to the wall again, both guns out and raised for action.

"Good kid!" he called. "I just made a trade with the fellers that stole your cattle. They can keep the steers, and we'll keep the poker winnin's I made by outcheating them two cheaters. Two hundred head at near thirty dollars apiece, kid—which gives you a bigger profit, an' saves you twelve hundred miles of trailin'. Watch the room, kid." He raised his hand. "Bartender, cash in them chips at five, ten an' fifty. *Pronto!*"

It did not take long to turn the counters into money, and Hopalong, backing past the table and toward his capable friend, picked up his winnings, jammed them into a pocket, and slowly reached the stair door.

"It's a tight corner, kid," said Hopalong crisply. "But yo're in no shape to ride. Up them stairs, in front of me." He stepped aside for his friend to pass, and then he stepped back again, his foot feeling for the first tread. His gaze flicked about the room, and he smiled thinly.

"My name's Cassidy," he said, and the smile now twisted his hard face. "My friends call me Hopalong. When I go to bed, I go to sleep. Any objections?"

The spellbound silence was broken by murmurs of surprise. Several faces showed quick friendliness, and a man in a far corner slowly got to his feet.

"An old friend of your'n is a right good friend of mine, Cassidy," he said, glancing slowly and significantly around the room. "Anybody that can't wait for daylight will taste my lead. Good night, you old hoss-thief!"

"Good night, friend," said Hopalong. The door slowly closed, and the crowd listened to the accented footsteps of a slightly lame, red-haired gentleman who made his unhurried way upward.

The man in the corner licked his lips and looked slowly around again.

"An' I meant what I said," he announced, and sat down to find his glass refilled.

Heroes Who Never Saw a White Hat

Mulford introduced Hopalong Cassidy to the world in 1907 in his first hardcover book, *Bar-20*. Throughout eighteen Bar-20 novels and even more short stories, Hopalong remained the same character. When *Short Stories* magazine asked Mulford for a Hopalong Cassidy story to print in their January 1930 issue, he sent them "Hopalong Sits In." As always, Hopalong turned out to be a tough, restless man, a man who is self-sufficient whether he is alone on the range or with strangers in a crowded saloon.

Hopalong believes in minding his own business, but he also has a lively curiosity. For example, when he realizes that the poker game is crooked, he decides to get into it. But not to "even up the odds" or to teach the cheaters a lesson. Hopalong is not morally offended by the situation; he is intrigued by it and joins the game in order to test his own skill.

Hopalong is never short on self-confidence. When he is sure what the game is, whether it is poker, a fist fight, or what Johnny Nelson calls a "Colt fandango," he nonchalantly plunges right on in. When it leads to trouble, as it usually does, Hopalong seems surprised.

He is not always reckless, however. When he hears about the plot to rustle the cattle, he decides to wait until he can learn more about it. Like all good poker players, he knows when to play his cards and when to wait for a better hand.

The backshooter, hoping to collect a hundred dollars for killing Cassidy, adds suspense to the story. Hopalong is fast, accurate, and cool when it comes to a gunfight, but none of that will help if a coward sneaks up and shoots him in the back. Hopalong doesn't even suspect anyone of wanting to kill him; as far as he knows, nobody in Trailville cares who he is.

In the end, we learn two more things about Hopalong Cassidy. He has a good sense of humor, as he shows when he announces that he has already "collected" the money for the stolen herd of cattle. And he has the right kind of friends; Johnny saves Hopalong from the ambusher, and the mysterious man in the far corner volunteers to stand guard while he and Johnny get a good night's rest.

Mulford said—more than once—that he didn't even recognize the movie version of Hopalong Cassidy. The man that he created in 1907 liked a good card game, a good drink, a good fight, and good companions. But he never wore a clean white hat.

Dorothy Johnson

1905–1984

Dorothy Johnson, a virtuoso of the western short story, wrote her way into the top ranks of that elite and significant group known as western women writers. Born in Iowa and raised in Montana, she began her literary career as a magazine editor in New York City. She eventually returned to Montana to live and write. While in New York, however, she became interested in the Plains Indian culture. Her intensive studies in eastern library collections gave her the background she needed in order to write two critically acclaimed collections of short stories: *Indian Country* and *The Hanging Tree*.

Three of Johnson's stories were made into successful films: *A Man Called Horse*, *The Hanging Tree*, and *The Man Who Shot Liberty Valance*. Her two powerful novels, *Buffalo Woman* and *All the Buffalo Returning*, are written from the Indian point of view and address the dilemmas facing Native Americans trying to exist in the white man's world.

Johnson's major themes include strength of character, which she had come to admire in frontier individuals; the clash between two powerful and determined cultures; and the influence of women upon the western frontier. Her work also shows a keen and subtle element of humor, an aspect of her own personality that could never be hidden.

Dorothy Johnson has been widely hailed as a major western writer. Judy Alter, in *Fifty Western Writers*, ascribes this to "the dignity she brings to the western through her affirmative belief in the strength of ordinary people."

Johnson was awarded the Western Writers of American Spur Award (1957), the Levi-Strauss Golden Saddleman Award (1976), the Western Heritage Wrangler Award (1978), and the Western Literature Association Distinguished Achievement Award (1981).

The Man Who Shot Liberty Valance

Bert Barricune died in 1910. Not more than a dozen persons showed up for his funeral. Among them was an earnest young reporter who hoped for a human-interest story; there were legends that the old man had been something of a gunfighter in the early days. A few aging men tiptoed in, singly or in pairs, scowling and edgy, clutching their battered hats—men who had been Bert's companions at drinking or penny ante while the world passed them by. One woman came, wearing a heavy veil that concealed her face. White and yellow streaks showed in her black-dyed hair. The reporter made a mental note: Old friend from the old District. But no story there—can't mention that.

One by one they filed past the casket, looking into the still face of old Bert Barricune, who had been nobody. His stubbly hair was white, and his lined face was as empty in death as his life had been. But death had added dignity.

One great spray of flowers spread behind the casket. The card read, "Senator and Mrs. Ransome Foster." There were no other flowers except, almost unnoticed, a few pale, leafless, pink and yellow blossoms scattered on the carpeted step. The reporter, squinting, finally identified them: son of a gun! Blossoms of the prickly pear. Cactus flowers. Seems suitable for the old man—flowers that grow on prairie wasteland. Well, they're free if you want to pick 'em, and Barricune's friends don't look prosperous. But how come the Senator sends a bouquet?

There was a delay, and the funeral director fidgeted a little, waiting. The reporter sat up straighter when he saw the last two mourners enter.

Senator Foster—sure, there's the crippled arm—and that must be his wife. Congress is still in session; he came all the way from Washington. Why would he bother, for an old wreck like Bert Barricune?

After the funeral was decently over, the reporter asked him. The Senator almost told the truth, but he caught himself in time. He said, "Bert Barricune was my friend for more than thirty years."

He could not give the true answer: He was my enemy; he was my conscience; he made me whatever I am.

Ransome Foster had been in the Territory for seven months when he ran into Liberty Valance. He had been afoot on the prairie for two days when he met Bert Barricune. Up to that time, Ranse Foster had been nobody in particular—a dude from the East, quietly inquisitive, moving from one shack town to another; just another tenderfoot with his own reasons for being there and no aim in life at all.

When Barricune found him on the prairie, Foster was indeed a tenderfoot. In his boots there was a warm, damp squidging where his feet had blistered, and the blisters had broken to bleed. He was bruised, sunburned, and filthy. He had been crawling, but when he saw Barricune riding toward him, he sat up. He had no horse, no saddle and, by that time, no pride.

Barricune looked down at him, not saying anything. Finally Ranse Foster asked, "Water?"

Barricune shook his head. "I don't carry none, but we can go where it is."

He stepped down from the saddle, a casual Samaritan, and with one heave pulled Foster upright.

"Git you in the saddle, can you stay there?" he inquired.

"If I can't," Foster answered through swollen lips, "shoot me."

Bert said amiably, "All right," and pulled the horse around. By twisting its ear, he held the animal quiet long enough to help the anguished stranger to the saddle. Then, on foot—and like any cowboy Bert Barricune hated walking—he led the horse five miles to the river. He let Foster lie where he fell in the cottonwood grove and brought him a hat full of water.

After that, Foster made three attempts to stand up. After the third failure, Barricune asked, grinning, "Want me to shoot you after all?"

"No," Foster answered. "There's something I want to do first."

Barricune looked at the bruises and commented, "Well, I should think so." He got on his horse and rode away. After an hour he returned with bedding and grub and asked, "Ain't you dead yet?"

The bruised and battered man opened his uninjured eye and said, "Not yet, but soon." Bert was amused. He brought a bucket of water and set up camp—a bedroll on a tarp, an armload of wood for a fire. He crouched on his heels while the tenderfoot, with cautious movements that told of pain, got his clothes off and splashed water on his body. No gunshot wounds, Barricune observed, but marks of kicks, and a couple that must have been made with a quirt.

After a while he asked, not inquisitively, but as one who has a right to know how matters stood, "Anybody looking for you?"

Foster rubbed dust from his clothes, being too full of pain to shake them. "No," he said. "But I'm looking for somebody."

"I ain't going to help you look," Bert informed him. "Town's over that way, two miles, when you get ready to come. Cache the stuff when you leave. I'll pick it up."

Three days later they met in the town marshal's office. They glanced at each other but did not speak. This time it was Bert Barricune who was bruised, though not much. The marshal was just letting him out of the one-cell jail when Foster limped into the office. Nobody said anything until Barricune, blinking and walking not quite steadily, had left. Foster saw him stop in front of the next building to speak to a girl. They walked away together, and it looked as if the young man were being scolded.

The marshal cleared his throat. "You wanted something, Mister?"

Foster answered, "Three men set me afoot on the prairie. Is that an offense against the law around here?"

The marshal eased himself and his stomach into a chair and frowned judiciously. "It ain't customary," he admitted. "Who was they?"

"The boss was a big man with black hair, dark eyes, and two gold teeth in front. The other two—"

"I know. Liberty Valance and a couple of his boys. Just what's your complaint, now?" Foster began to understand that no help was going to come from the marshal.

"They rob you?" the marshal asked.

"They didn't search me."

"Take your gun?"

"I didn't have one."

"Steal your horse?"

"Gave him a crack with a quirt, and he left."

"Saddle on him?"

"No. I left it out there."

The marshal shook his head. "Can't see you got any legal complaint," he said with relief. "Where was this?"

"On a road in the woods, by a creek. Two days' walk from here."

The marshal got to his feet. "You don't even know what jurisdiction it was in. They knocked you around; well, that could happen. Man gets in a fight—could happen to anybody."

Foster said dryly, "Thanks a lot."

The marshal stopped him as he reached the door. "There's a reward for Liberty Valance."

"I still haven't got a gun," Foster said. "Does he come here often?"

"Nope. Nothing he'd want in Twotrees. Hard man to find." The marshall looked Foster up and down. "He won't come after you here." It was as if he had added, *Sonny!* "Beat you up once, he won't come again for that."

And I, Foster realized, am not man enough to go after him.

"Fact is," the marshal added, "I can't think of any bait that would bring him in. Pretty quiet here. Yes sir." He put his thumbs in his galluses and looked out the window, taking credit for the quietness.

Bait, Foster thought. He went out thinking about it. For the first time in a couple of years he had an ambition—not a laudable one, but something to aim at. He was going to be the bait for Liberty Valance and, as far as he could be, the trap as well.

At the Elite Cafe he stood meekly in the doorway, hat in hand, like a man who expects and deserves to be refused anything he might ask for. Clearing his throat, he asked, "Could I work for a meal?"

The girl who was filling sugar bowls looked up and pitied him. "Why, I should think so. Mr. Anderson!" She was the girl who had walked away with Barricune, scolding him.

The proprietor came from the kitchen, and Ranse Foster repeated his question, cringing, but with a suggestion of a sneer.

"Go around back and split some wood," Anderson answered, turning back to the kitchen.

"He could just as well eat first," the waitress suggested. "I'll dish up some stew to begin with."

Ranse ate fast, as if he expected the plate to be snatched away. He knew the girl glanced at him several times, and he hated her for it. He had not counted on anyone's pitying him in his new role of sneering humility, but he knew he might as well get used to it.

When she brought his pie, she said, "If you was looking for a job . . ."

He forced himself to look at her suspiciously. "Yes?"

"You could try the Prairie Belle. I heard they needed a swamper."

Bart Barricune, riding out to the river camp for his bedroll, hardly knew the man he met there. Ranse Foster was haughty, condescending, and cringing all at once. He spoke with a faint sneer, and stood as if he expected to be kicked.

"I assumed you'd be back for your belongings," he said. "I realized that you would change your mind."

Barricune, strapping up his bedroll, looked blank. "Never changed it," he disagreed. "Doing just what I planned. I never give you my bedroll."

"Of course not, of course not," the new Ranse Foster agreed with sneering humility. "It's yours. You have every right to reclaim it."

Barricune looked at him narrowly and hoisted the bedroll to sling it up behind his saddle. "I should have left you for the buzzards," he remarked.

Foster agreed, with a smile that should have got him a fist in the teeth. "Thank you, my friend," he said with no gratitude. "Thank you for all your kindness, which I have done nothing to deserve and shall do nothing to repay."

Barricune rode off, scowling, with the memory of his good deed irritating him like lice. The new Foster followed, far behind, on foot.

Sometimes in later life Ranse Foster thought of the several men he had been through the years. He did not admire any of them very much. He was by no means ashamed of the man he finally became, except that he owed too much to other people. One man he had been when he was young, a serious student, gullible and quick-tempered. Another man had been reckless and without an aim; he went West, with two thousand dollars of his own, after a quarrel with the executor of his father's estate. That man did not last long. Liberty Valance had whipped him with a quirt and kicked him into unconsciousness, for no reason except that Liberty, meeting him and knowing him for a tenderfoot, was able to do so. That man died on the prairie. After that, there was the man who set out to be the bait that would bring Liberty Valance into Twotrees.

Ranse Foster had never hated anyone before he met Liberty Valance, but Liberty was not the last man he learned to hate. He hated the man he himself had been while he waited to meet Liberty again.

The swamper's job at the Prairie Belle was not disgraceful until Ranse Foster made it so. When he swept floors, he was so obviously contemptuous of the work and of himself for doing it that other men saw him as contemptible. He watched the customers with a curled lip as if they were beneath him. But when a poker player threw a white chip on the floor, the swamper looked at him with half-veiled hatred—and picked up the chip. They talked about him at the Prairie Belle, because he could not be ignored.

At the end of the first month, he bought a Colt .45 from a drunken cowboy who needed money worse than he needed two guns. After that, Ranse went without part of his sleep in order to walk out, seven mornings a week, to where his first camp had been and practice target shooting. And the second time he overslept from exhaustion, Joe Mosten of the Prairie Belle fired him.

"Here's your pay," Joe growled, and dropped the money on the floor.

A week passed before he got another job. He ate his meals frugally in the Elite Cafe and let himself be seen stealing scraps off plates that other diners had left. Lillian, the older of the two waitresses, yelled her disgust, but Hallie, who was young, pitied him.

"Come to the back door when it's dark," she murmured, "and I'll give you a bite. There's plenty to spare."

The second evening he went to the back door, Bert Barricune was there ahead of him. He said gently, "Hallie is my girl."

"No offense intended," Foster answered. "The young lady offered me food, and I have come to get it."

"A dog eats where it can," young Barricune drawled.

Ranse's muscles tensed and rage mounted in his throat, but he caught himself in time and shrugged. Bert said something then that scared him: "If you wanted to get talked about, it's working fine. They're talking clean over in Dunbar."

"What they do or say in Dunbar," Foster answered, "is nothing to me."

"It's where Liberty Valance hangs out," the other man said casually. "In case you care."

Ranse almost confided then, but instead said stiffly, "I do not quite appreciate your strange interest in my affairs."

Barricune pushed back his hat and scratched his head. "I don't understand it myself. But leave my girl alone."

"As charming as Miss Hallie may be," Ranse told him, "I am interested only in keeping my stomach filled."

"Then why don't you work for a living? The clerk at Dowitts' quit this afternoon."

Jake Dowitt hired him as a clerk because nobody else wanted the job.

"Read and write, do you?" Dowitt asked. "Work with figures?"

Foster drew himself up. "Sir, whatever may be said against me, I believe I may lay claim to being a scholar. That much I claim, if nothing more. I have read law."

"Maybe the job ain't good enough for you," Dowitt suggested.

Foster became humble again. "Any job is good enough for me. I will also sweep the floor."

"You will also keep up the fire in the stove," Dowitt told him. "Seven in the morning till nine at night. Got a place to live?"

"I sleep in the livery stable in return for keeping it shoveled out."

Dowitt had intended to house his clerk in a small room over the store, but he changed his mind. "Got a shed out back you can bunk in," he offered. "You'll have to clean it out first. Used to keep chickens there."

"There is one thing," Foster said. "I want two half-days off a week."

Dowitt looked over the top of his spectacles. "Now what would you do with time off? Never mind. You can have it—for less pay. I give you a discount on what you buy in the store."

The only purchase Foster made consisted of four boxes of cartridges a week.

In the store, he weighed salt pork as if it were low stuff but himself still lower, humbly measured lengths of dress goods for the women customers. He added vanity to his other unpleasantnesses and let customers discover him combing his hair admiringly before a small mirror. He let himself be seen reading a small black book, which aroused curiosity.

It was while he worked at the store that he started Twotrees' first school. Hallie was responsible for that. Handing him a plate heaped higher than other customers got at the café, she said gently, "You're a learned man, they say, Mr. Foster."

With Hallie he could no longer sneer or pretend humility, for Hallie was herself humble, as well as gentle and kind. He protected himself from her by not speaking unless he had to.

He answered, "I have had advantages, Miss Hallie, before fate brought me here."

"That book you read," she asked wistfully, "what's it about?"

"It was written by a man named Plato," Ranse told her stiffly. "It was written in Greek."

She brought him a cup of coffee, hesitated for a moment and then asked, "You can read and write American, too, can't you?"

"English, Miss Hallie," he corrected. "English is our mother tongue. I am quite familiar with English."

She put her red hands on the café counter. "Mr. Foster," she whispered, "will you teach me to read?"

He was too startled to think of an answer she could not defeat.

"Bert wouldn't like it," he said. "You're a grown woman besides. It wouldn't look right for you to be learning to read now."

She shook her head. "I can't learn any younger." She sighed. "I always wanted to know how to read and write." She walked away toward the kitchen, and Ranse Foster was struck with an emotion he knew he could not afford. He was swept with pity. He called her back.

"Miss Hallie. Not you alone—people would talk about you. But if you brought Bert—"

"Bert can already read some. He don't care about it. But there's some kids in town." Her face was so lighted that Ranse looked away.

He still tried to escape. "Won't you be ashamed, learning with children?"

"Why, I'll be proud to learn any way at all," she said.

He had three little girls, two restless little boys, and Hallie in Twotrees' first school session—one hour each afternoon, in Dowitt's storeroom. Dowitt did not dock his pay for the time spent, but he puzzled a great deal. So did the children's parents. The children themselves were puzzled at some of the things he read aloud, but they were patient. After all, lessons lasted only an hour.

"When you are older, you will understand this," he promised, not looking at Hallie, and then he read Shakespeare's sonnet that begins:

No longer mourn for me when I am dead
Than you shall hear the surly sullen bell

and ends:

Do not so much as my poor name rehearse,
But let your love even with my life decay,
  Lest the wise world should look into your moan
  And mock you with me after I am gone.

Hallie understood the warning, he knew. He read another sonnet, too:

When in disgrace with Fortune and men's eyes,
I all alone beweep my outcast state,

and carefully did not look up at her as he finished it:

For thy sweet love rememb'red such wealth brings
That then I scorn to change my state with kings.

Her earnestness in learning was distasteful to him—the anxious way she grasped a pencil and formed letters, the little gasp with which she always began to read aloud. Twice he made her cry, but she never missed a lesson.

He wished he had a teacher for his own learning, but he could not trust anyone, and so he did his lessons alone. Bert Barricune caught him at it on one of those free afternoons when Foster, on a horse from the livery stable, had ridden miles out of town to a secluded spot.

Ranse Foster had an empty gun in his hand when Barricune stepped out from behind a sandstone column and remarked, "I've seen better."

Foster whirled, and Barricune added, "I could have been somebody else—and your gun's empty."

"When I see somebody else, it won't be," Foster promised.

"If you'd asked me," Barricune mused, "I could've helped you. But you didn't want no helping. A man shouldn't be ashamed to ask somebody that knows better than him." His gun was suddenly in his hand, and five shots cracked their echoes around the skull-white sandstone pillars. Half an inch above each of five cards that Ranse had tacked to a dead tree, at the level of a man's waist, a splintered hole appeared in the wood. "Didn't want to spoil your targets," Barricune explained.

"I'm not ashamed to ask you," Foster told him angrily, "since you know so much. I shoot straight but slow. I'm asking you now."

Barricune, reloading his gun, shook his head. "It's kind of late for that. I come out to tell you that Liberty Valance is in town. He's interested in the dude that anybody can kick around—this here tenderfoot that boasts how he can read Greek."

"Well," said Foster softly. "Well, so the time has come."

"Don't figure you're riding into town with me," Bert warned. "You're coming all by yourself."

Ranse rode into town with his gun belt buckled on. Always before, he had carried it wrapped in a slicker. In town, he allowed himself the luxury of one last vanity. He went to the barbershop, neither sneering nor cringing, and said sharply, "Cut my hair. Short."

The barber was nervous, but he worked understandingly fast.

"Thought you was partial to that long wavy hair of yourn," he remarked.

"I don't know why you thought so," Foster said coldly.

Out in the street again, he realized that he did not know how to go about the job. He did not know where Liberty Valance was, and he was determined not to be caught like a rat. He intended to look for Liberty.

Joe Mosten's right-hand man was lounging at the door of the Prairie Belle. He moved over to bar the way.

"Not in there, Foster," he said gently. It was the first time in months that Ranse Foster had heard another man address him respectfully. His presence was recognized—as a menace to the fixtures of the Prairie Belle.

When I die, sometime today, he thought, they won't say I was a coward. They may say I was a damn fool, but I won't care by that time.

"Where is he?" Ranse asked.

"I couldn't tell you that," the man said apologetically. "I'm young and healthy, and where he is is none of my business. Joe'd be obliged if you stay out of the bar, that's all."

Ranse looked across toward Dowitt's store. The padlock was on the door. He glanced north, toward the marshal's office.

"That's closed, too," the saloon man told him courteously. "Marshal was called out of town an hour ago."

Ranse threw back his head and laughed. The sound echoed back from the false-fronted buildings across the street. There was nobody walking in the street; there were not even any horses tied to the hitching racks.

"Send Liberty word," he ordered in the tone of one who has a right to command. "Tell him the tenderfoot wants to see him again."

The saloon man cleared his throat. "Guess it won't be necessary. That's him coming down at the end of the street, wouldn't you say?"

Ranse looked, knowing the saloon man was watching him curiously.

"I'd say it is," he agreed. "Yes, I'd say that was Liberty Valance."

"I'll be going inside now," the other man remarked apologetically. "Well, take care of yourself." He was gone without a sound.

This is the classic situation, Ranse realized. Two enemies walking to meet each other along the dusty, waiting street of a western town. What reasons other men have had, I will never know. There are so many things I have never learned! And now there is no time left.

He was an actor who knew the end of the scene but had forgotten the lines and never knew the cue for them. One of us ought to say something, he realized. I should have planned this all out in advance. But all I ever saw was the end of it.

Liberty Valance, burly and broad-shouldered, walked stiff-legged, with his elbows bent.

When he is close enough for me to see whether he is smiling, Ranse Foster thought, somebody's got to speak.

He looked into his own mind and realized, This man is afraid, this Ransome Foster. But nobody else knows it. He walks and is afraid, but he is no coward. Let them remember that. Let Hallie remember that.

Liberty Valance gave the cue. "Looking for me?" he called between his teeth. He was grinning.

Ranse was almost grateful to him; it was as if Liberty had said, The time is now!

"I owe you something," Ranse answered. "I want to pay my debt."

Liberty's hand flashed with his own. The gun in Foster's hand exploded, and so did the whole world.

Two shots to my one, he thought—his last thought for a while.

He looked up at a strange, unsteady ceiling and a face that wavered like a reflection in water. The bed beneath him swung even after he closed his eyes. Far away some one said, "Shove some more cloth in the wound. It slows the bleeding."

He knew with certain agony where the wound was—in his right shoulder. When they touched it, he heard himself cry out.

The face that wavered above him was a new one. Bert Barricune's.

"He's dead," Barricune said.

Foster answered from far away, "I am not."

Barricune said, "I didn't mean you."

Ranse turned his head away from the pain, and the face that had shivered above him before was Hallie's, white and big-eyed. She put a hesitant hand on his, and he was annoyed to see that hers was trembling.

"Are you shaking," he asked, "because there's blood on my hands?"

"No," she answered. "It's because they might have been getting cold."

He was aware then that other people were in the room; they stirred and moved aside as the doctor entered.

"Maybe you're gonna keep that arm," the doctor told him at last. "But it's never gonna be much use to you."

The trial was held three weeks after the shooting, in the hotel room where Ranse lay in bed. The charge was disturbing the peace; he pleaded guilty and was fined ten dollars.

When the others had gone, he told Bert Barricune, "There was a reward, I heard. That would pay the doctor and the hotel."

"You ain't going to collect it," Bert informed him. "It'd make you too big for your britches." Barricune sat looking at him for a moment and then remarked, "You didn't kill Liberty."

Foster frowned. "They buried him."

"Liberty fired once. You fired once and missed. I fired once, and I don't generally miss. I ain't going to collect the reward, neither. Hallie don't hold with violence."

Foster said thoughtfully, "That was all I had to be proud of."

"You faced him," Barricune said. "You went to meet him. If you got to be proud of something, you can remember that. It's a fact you ain't got much else."

Ranse looked at him with narrowed eyes. "Bert, are you a friend of mine?"

Bert smiled without humor. "You know I ain't. I picked you up off the prairie, but I'd do that for the lowest scum that crawls. I wisht I hadn't."

"Then why—"

Bert looked at the toe of his boot. "Hallie likes you. I'm a friend of Hallie's. That's all I ever will be, long as you're around."

Ranse said, "Then I shot Liberty Valance." That was the nearest he ever dared coming to saying "Thank you." And that was when Bert Barricune started being his conscience, his Nemesis, his lifelong enemy and the man who made him great.

"Would she be happy living back East?" Foster asked. "There's money waiting for me there if I go back."

Bert answered, "What do you think?" He stood up and stretched. "You got quite a problem, ain't you? You could solve it easy by just going back alone. There ain't much a man can do here with a crippled arm."

He went out and shut the door behind him.

There is always a way out, Foster thought, if a man wants to take it. Bert had been his way out when he met Liberty on the street of Twotrees. To go home was the way out of this.

I learned to live without pride, he told himself. I could learn to forget about Hallie.

When she came, between the dinner dishes and setting the tables for supper at the café, he told her.

She did not cry. Sitting in the chair beside his bed, she winced and jerked one hand in protest when he said, "As soon as I can travel, I'll be going back where I came from."

She did not argue. She said only, "I wish you good luck, Ransome. Bert and me, we'll look after you long as you stay. And remember you after you're gone."

"How will you remember me?" he demanded harshly.

As his student she had been humble, but as a woman she had her pride. "Don't ask that," she said, and got up from the chair.

"Hallie, Hallie," he pleaded, "how can I stay? How can I earn a living?"

She said indignantly, as if someone else had insulted him, "Ranse Foster, I just guess you could do anything you wanted to."

"Hallie," he said gently, "sit down."

He never really wanted to be outstanding. He had two aims in life: to make Hallie happy and to keep Bert Barricune out of trouble. He defended Bert on charges ranging from drunkenness to stealing cattle, and Bert served time twice.

Ranse Foster did not want to run for judge, but Bert remarked, "I think Hallie would kind of like it if you was His Honor." Hallie was pleased but not surprised when he was elected. Ranse was surprised but not pleased.

He was not eager to run for the legislature—that was after the territory became a state—but there was Bert Barricune in the background, never urging, never advising, but watching with half-closed, bloodshot eyes. Bert Barricune, who never amounted to anything, but never intruded, was a living, silent reminder of three debts: a hat full of water under the cottonwoods, gunfire in a dusty street, and Hallie, quietly sewing beside a lamp in the parlor. And the Fosters had four sons.

All the things the opposition said about Ranse Foster when he ran for the state legislature were true, except one. He had been a lowly swamper in a frontier saloon; he had been a dead beat, accepting handouts at the alley entrance of a café; he had been despicable and despised. But the accusation that lost him the election was false. He had not killed Liberty Valance. He never served in the state legislature.

When there was talk of his running for governor, he refused. Handy Strong, who knew politics, tried to persuade him.

"That shooting, we'll get around that. 'The Honorable Ransome Foster walked down a street in broad daylight to meet an enemy of society. He shot him down in a fair fight, of necessity, the way you'd shoot a mad dog—but Liberty Valance could shoot back, and he did. Ranse Foster carries the mark of that encounter today in a crippled right arm. He is still paying the price for protecting law-abiding citizens. And he was the first teacher west of Rosy Buttes. He served without pay.' You've come a long way, Ranse, and you're going further."

"A long way," Foster agreed, "for a man who never wanted to go anywhere. I don't want to be governor."

When Handy had gone, Bert Barricune sagged in, unwashed, unshaven. He sat down stiffly. At the age of fifty, he was an old man, an unwanted relic of the frontier that was gone, a legacy to more civilized times that had no place for him. He filled his pipe deliberately. After a while he remarked. "The other side is gonna say you ain't fitten to be governor. Because your wife ain't fancy enough. They're gonna say Hallie didn't even learn to read till she was growed up."

Ranse was on his feet, white with fury. "Then I'm going to win this election if it kills me."

"I don't reckon it'll kill you," Bert drawled. "Liberty Valance couldn't."

"I could have got rid of the weight of that affair long ago," Ranse reminded him, "by telling the truth."

"You could yet," Bert answered. "Why don't you?"

Ranse said bitterly, "Because I owe you too much. . . . I don't think Hallie wants to be the governor's lady. She's shy."

"Hallie don't never want nothing for herself. She wants things for you. The way I feel, I wouldn't mourn at your funeral. But what Hallie wants, I'm gonna try to see she gets."

"So am I," Ranse promised grimly.

"Then I don't mind telling you," Bert admitted, "that it was me reminded the opposition to dig up that matter of how she couldn't read."

As the Senator and his wife rode out to the airport after old Bert Barricune's barren funeral, Hallie sighed. "Bert never had much of anything. I guess he never wanted much."

He wanted you to be happy, Ranse Foster thought, and he did the best he knew how.

"I wonder where those prickly-pear blossoms came from," he mused.

Hallie glanced up at him, smiling. "From me," she said.

The Man Who Wanted to Be Nobody

This story will fool you. Dorothy Johnson avoids elaborate descriptions and long, drawn-out explanations of the events. Her characters are easy to understand, almost as if they were "stock" characters. But underneath the simplicity there are complex motivations and a three-way relationship with very subtle complications.

When writers use "stock" characters and situations, it is as if they just reach into a box and take out the one they want. The problem is that we get used to seeing stock villains beat up standard tenderfeet, and then we might forget to imagine what it would really be like to be bullied and threatened and kicked and quirted by a terrifying bully like Liberty Valance. A beating like that could literally change a person's whole life, as it does in the case of Ranse Foster.

Foster, who is nobody in particular, suddenly finds himself pretending to believe that he *is* somebody—a "boasting tenderfoot." Then two other nobodies, Barricune and Hallie, find themselves involved in Foster's life.

These latter two are realists: they know what their roles are in the little western town. But after Foster arrives, Hallie starts to want something better for herself, and so she learns to read. Barricune begins to want her to be happy, and so he in turn pushes Foster to become more than he is, more than he really wants to be. Barricune is Foster's "silent reminder of three debts: a hat full of water under the cottonwoods, gunfire in a dusty street, and Hallie."

Liberty Valance's name is interesting. "Liberty" has quite a few implications, because Barricune kills Foster's liberty, in a way. But the word "valence" also refers to the cause—and the effect—of the gunfight. Foster *could* be thinking of Liberty Valance *or* Bert Barricune when he says, "He was my enemy; he was my conscience; he made me whatever I am." According to my dictionary, valence is the capacity to unite, react, or interact with something else.

And that's what the shooting of Liberty Valance does for Ranse Foster. It tests his capacity to interact, his ability to understand how conscience and motivation can come in many forms. Because of those few seconds of gunfire, he goes a long way. "'A long way,' Foster agreed, 'for a man who never wanted to go anywhere.'"

Luke Short

(Frederick D. Glidden)

1908–1975

After a brief career in journalism, Fred Glidden was quoted as saying, "I've read or heard that all newspapermen are disappointed writers, but in me you behold a writer who is a disappointed newspaperman. I've been fired from more newspapers than I like to remember, even if I could."

What journalism missed by not keeping him on the job, western fiction gained a hundredfold. Between 1936 and 1975, he wrote fifty-one western novels and became known as the "Dean of Western Writers." Adaptations of his stories were made into such films as *Ramrod*, *Coroner Creek*, *Station West*, *Blood on the Moon*, *Ambush*, *Vengeance Valley*, *Silver City*, *Ride the Man Down*, and *Hell's Outpost*.

Glidden is renowned for fast-moving story lines, for authentic portraits of life in frontier towns, and for heroes and heroines who confront the lawlessness of the frontier. Russell Nye, in his critical overview of the western, *The Unembarrassed Muse*, says that Luke Short is "the best of action-packed writers."

The pen name "Luke Short" was suggested to Frederick Glidden by his agent. The original Luke Short (1854–1893) was a gambler who fraternized with the famous and the infamous of Dodge City in its heyday, including the Earps, Doc Holliday, and Bat Masterson.

Top Hand

Gus Irby was out on the boardwalk in front of the Elite, giving his swamper hell for staving in an empty beer barrel, when the kid passed on his way to the feed stable. His horse was a good one and it was tired, Gus saw, and the kid had a little hump in his back from the cold of a mountain October morning. In spite of the ample layer of flesh that Gus wore carefully like an uncomfortable shroud, he shivered in his shirt sleeves and turned into the saloon, thinking without much interest *Another fiddlefooted dry-country kid that's been paid off after round-up.*

Later, while he was taking out the cash for the day and opening up some fresh cigars, Gus saw the kid go into the Pride Café for breakfast, and afterward come out, toothpick in mouth, and cruise both sides of Wagon Mound's main street in aimless curiosity.

After that, Gus wasn't surprised when he looked around at the sound of the door opening, and saw the kid coming toward the bar. He was in a clean and faded shirt and looked as if he'd been cold for a good many hours. Gus said good morning and took down his best whisky and a glass and put them in front of the kid.

"First customer in the morning gets a drink on the house," Gus announced.

"Now I know why I rode all night," the kid said, and he grinned at Gus. He was a pleasant-faced kid with pale eyes that weren't shy or sullen or bold, and maybe because of this he didn't fit readily into any of Gus' handy character pigeonholes. Gus had seen them young and fiddlefooted before, but they were the tough kids, and for a man with no truculence in him, like Gus, talking with them was like trying to pet a tiger.

Gus leaned against the back bar and watched the kid take his whisky and wipe his mouth on his sleeve, and Gus found himself getting curious. Half a lifetime of asking skillful questions that didn't seem like questions at all, prompted Gus to observe now, "If you're goin' on through you better pick up a coat. This high country's cold now."

"I figure this is far enough," the kid said.

"Oh, well, if somebody sent for you, that's different." Gus reached around lazily for a cigar.

The kid pulled out a silver dollar from his pocket and put it on the bar top, and then poured himself another whisky, which Gus was sure he didn't want, but which courtesy dictated he should buy. "Nobody sent for me, either," the kid observed. "I ain't got any money."

Gus picked up the dollar and got change from the cash drawer and put it in front of the kid, afterward lighting his cigar. This was when the announcement came.

"I'm a top hand," the kid said quietly, looking levelly at Gus. "Who's lookin' for one?"

Gus was glad he was still lighting his cigar, else he might have smiled. If there had been a third man here, Gus would have winked at him surreptitiously; but since there wasn't, Gus kept his face expressionless, drew on his cigar a moment, and then observed gently, "You look pretty young for a top hand."

"The best cow pony I ever saw was four years old," the kid answered pointedly.

Gus smiled faintly and shook his head. "You picked a bad time. Round-up's over."

The kid nodded, and drank down his second whisky quickly, waited for his breath to come normally. Then he said, "Much obliged. I'll see you again," and turned toward the door.

A mild cussedness stirred within Gus, and after a moment's hesitation he called out, "Wait a minute."

The kid hauled up and came back to the bar. He moved with an easy grace that suggested quickness and work-hardened muscle, and for a moment Gus, a careful man, was undecided. But the kid's face, so young and without caution, reassured him, and he folded his heavy arms on the bar top and pulled his nose thoughtfully. "You figure to hit all the outfits, one by one, don't you?"

The kid nodded, and Gus frowned and was silent a moment, and then he murmured, almost to himself, "I had a notion—oh, hell, I don't know."

"Go ahead," the kid said, and then his swift grin came again. "I'll try anything once."

"Look," Gus said, as if his mind were made up. "We got a newspaper here—the Wickford County Free Press. Comes out every Thursday, that's today." He looked soberly at the kid. "Whyn't you put a piece in there and say 'Top hand wants a job at forty dollars a month'? Tell 'em what you can do and tell 'em to come see you here if they want a hand. They'll all get it in a couple days. That way you'll save yourself a hundred miles of ridin'. Won't cost much either."

The kid thought awhile and then asked, without smiling, "Where's this newspaper at?"

Gus told him and the kid went out. Gus put the bottle away and doused the glass in water, and he was smiling slyly at his thoughts. Wait till the boys read that in the Free Press. They were going to have some fun with that kid, Gus reflected.

Johnny McSorley stepped out into the chill thin sunshine. The last silver dollar in his pants pocket was a solid weight against his leg, and he was aware that he'd probably spend it in the next few minutes on the newspaper piece. He wondered about that, and figured shrewdly it had an off chance of working.

Four riders dismounted at a tie rail ahead and paused a moment, talking. Johnny looked them over and picked out their leader, a tall, heavy, scowling man in his middle thirties who was wearing a mackinaw unbuttoned.

Johnny stopped and said, "You know anybody lookin' for a top hand?" and grinned pleasantly at the big man.

For a second Johnny thought he was going to smile. He didn't think he'd have liked the smile, once he saw it, but the man's face settled into the scowl again. "I never saw a top hand that couldn't vote," he said.

Johnny looked at him carefully, not smiling, and said, "Look at one now, then," and went on, and by the time he'd taken two steps he thought, *Voted, huh? A man must grow pretty slow in this high country.*

He crossed the street and paused before a window marked WICKFORD COUNTY FREE PRESS. JOB PRINTING D. MELAVEN, ED. AND PROP. He went inside, then. A girl was seated at a cluttered desk, staring at the street, tapping a pencil against her teeth. Johnny tramped over to her, noting the infernal racket made by one of two men at a small press under the lamp behind the railed-off office space.

Johnny said "Hello," and the girl turned tiredly and said, "Hello, bub." She had on a plain blue dress with a high bodice and a narrow lace collar, and she was a very pretty girl, but tired, Johnny noticed. Her long yellow hair was worn in braids that crossed almost atop her head, and she looked, Johnny thought, like a small kid who has pinned her hair up out of the way for her Saturday night bath. He thought all this and then remembered her greeting, and he reflected without rancor, *Damn, that's twice,* and he said, "I got a piece for the paper, sis."

"Don't call me sis," the girl said. "Anybody's name I don't know, I call him bub. No offense. I got that from pa, I guess."

That's likely, Johnny thought, and he said amiably, "Any girl's name I don't know, I call her sis. I got that from ma."

The cheerful effrontery of the remark widened the girl's eyes. She held out her hand now and said with dignity, "Give it to me. I'll see it gets in next week."

"That's too late," Johnny said. "I got to get it in this week."

"Why?"

"I ain't got money enough to hang around another week."

The girl stared carefully at him. "What is it?"

"I want to put a piece in about myself. I'm a top hand, and I'm lookin' for work. The fella over there at the saloon says why don't I put a piece in the paper about wantin' work, instead of ridin' out lookin' for it."

The girl was silent a full five seconds and then said, "You don't look that simple. Gus was having fun with you."

"I figured that," Johnny agreed. "Still, it might work. If you're caught short-handed, you take anything."

The girl shook her head. "It's too late. The paper's made up." Her voice was meant to hold a note of finality, but Johnny regarded her curiously, with a maddening placidity.

"You D. Melaven?" he asked.

"No. That's pa."

"Where's he?"

"Back there. Busy."

Johnny saw the gate in the rail that separated the office from the shop and he headed toward it. He heard the girl's chair scrape on the floor and her urgent command, "Don't go back there. It's not allowed."

Johnny looked over his shoulder and grinned and said, "I'll try anything once," and went on through the gate, hearing the girl's swift steps behind him. He halted alongside a square-built and solid man with a thatch of stiff hair more gray than black, and said, "You D. Melaven?"

"Dan Melaven, bub. What can I do for you?"

That's three times, Johnny thought, and he regarded Melaven's square face without anger. He liked the face; it was homely and stubborn and intelligent, and the eyes were both sharp and kindly. Hearing the girl stop beside him, Johnny said, "I got a piece for the paper today."

The girl put in quickly, "I told him it was too late, pa. Now you tell him, and maybe he'll get out."

"Cassie," Melaven said in surprised protest.

"I don't care. We can't unlock the forms for every out-at-the-pants puncher that asks us. Besides, I think he's one of Alec Barr's bunch." She spoke vehemently, angrily, and Johnny listened to her with growing amazement.

"Alec who?" he asked.

"I saw you talking to him, and then you came straight over here from him," Cassie said hotly.

"I hit him for work."

"I don't believe it."

"Cassie," Melaven said grimly, "come back here a minute." He took her by the arm and led her toward the back of the shop, where they halted and engaged in a quiet, earnest conversation.

Johnny shook his head in bewilderment, and then looked around him. The biggest press, he observed, was idle. And on a stone-topped table where Melaven had been working was a metal form almost filled with lines of type and gray metal pieces of assorted sizes and shapes. Now, Johnny McSorley did not know any more than the average person about the workings of a newspaper, but his common sense told him that Cassie had lied to him when she said it was too late to accept his advertisement. Why, there was space and to spare in that form for the few lines of type his message would need. Turning this over in his mind, he wondered what was behind her refusal.

Presently, the argument settled, Melaven and Cassie came back to him, and Johnny observed that Cassie, while chastened, was still mad.

"All right, what do you want printed, bub?" Melaven asked.

Johnny told him and Melaven nodded when he was finished, said, "Pay her," and went over to the type case.

Cassie went back to the desk and Johnny followed her, and when she was seated he said, "What do I owe you?"

Cassie looked speculatively at him, her face still flushed with anger. "How much money have you got?"

"A dollar some."

"It'll be two dollars," Cassie said.

Johnny pulled out his silver dollar and put it on the desk. "You print it just the same; I'll be back with the rest later."

Cassie said with open malice, "You'd have it now, bub, if you hadn't been drinking before ten o'clock."

Johnny didn't do anything for a moment, and then he put both hands on the desk and leaned close to her. "How old are you?" he asked quietly.

"Seventeen."

"I'm older'n you," Johnny murmured. "So the next time you call me 'bub' I'm goin' to take down your pigtails and pull 'em. I'll try anything once."

Once he was in the sunlight, crossing toward the Elite, he felt better. He smiled—partly at himself but mostly at Cassie. She was a real spitfire, kind of pretty and kind of nice, and he wished he knew what her father said to her that made her so mad, and why she'd been mad in the first place.

Gus was breaking out a new case of whisky and stacking bottles against the back mirror as Johnny came in and went up to the bar. Neither of them spoke while Gus finished, and Johnny gazed absently at the poker game at one of the tables and now yawned sleepily.

Gus said finally, "You get it in all right?"

Johnny nodded thoughtfully and said, "She mad like that at everybody?"

"Who? Cassie?"

"First she didn't want to take the piece, but her old man made her. Then she charges me more for it than I got in my pocket. Then she combs me over like I got my head stuck in the cookie crock for drinkin' in the morning. She calls me bub, to boot."

"She calls everybody bub."

"Not me no more," Johnny said firmly, and yawned again.

Gus grinned and sauntered over to the cash box. When he came back he put ten silver dollars on the bar top and said, "Pay me back when you get your job. And I got rooms upstairs if you want to sleep."

Johnny grinned. "Sleep, hunh? I'll try anything once." He took the money, said "Much obliged" and started away from the bar and then paused. "Say, who's this Alec Barr?"

Johnny saw Gus's eyes shift swiftly to the poker game and then shuttle back to him. Gus didn't say anything.

"See you later," Johnny said.

He climbed the stairs whose entrance was at the end of the bar, wondering why Gus was so careful about Alec Barr.

A gunshot somewhere out in the street woke him. The sun was gone from the room, so it must be afternoon, he thought. He pulled on his boots, slopped some water into the washbowl and washed up, pulled a hand across his cheek and decided he should shave, and went downstairs. There wasn't anybody in the saloon, not even behind the bar. On the tables and on the bar top, however, were several newspapers, all fresh. He was reminded at once that he was in debt to the Wickford County Free Press for the sum of one dollar. He pulled one of the newspapers toward him and turned to the page where all the advertisements were.

When, after some minutes, he finished, he saw that his advertisement was not there. A slow wrath grew in him as he thought of the girl and her father taking his money, and when it had come to full flower, he went out of the Elite and cut across toward the newspaper office. He saw, without really noticing it, the group of men clustered in front of the store across from the newspaper office. He swung under the tie rail and reached the opposite boardwalk just this side of the newspaper office and a man who was lounging against the building. He was a puncher and when he saw Johnny heading up the walk he said, "Don't go across there."

Johnny said grimly, "You stop me," and went on, and he heard the puncher say, "All right, getcher head blown off."

His boots crunched broken glass in front of the office and he came to a gingerly halt, looking down at his feet. His glance raised to the window, and he saw where there was a big jag of glass out of the window, neatly wiping out the Wickford except for the W on the sign and ribboning cracks to all four corners of the frame. His surprise held him motionless for a moment, and then he heard a voice calling from across the street, "Clear out of there, son."

That makes four times, Johnny thought resignedly, and he glanced across the street and saw Alec Barr, several men clotted around him, looking his way.

Johnny went on and turned into the newspaper office and it was like walking into a dark cave. The lamp was extinguished.

And then he saw the dim forms of Cassie Melaven and her father back of the railing beside the job press, and the reason for his errand came back to him with a rush. Walking through the gate, he began firmly, "I got a dollar owed—" and ceased talking and halted abruptly. There was a six-shooter in Dan Melaven's hand hanging at his side. Johnny looked at it, and then raised his glance to Melaven's face and found the man watching him with a bitter amusement in his eyes. His glance shuttled to Cassie, and she was looking at him as if she didn't see him, and her face seemed very pale in that gloom. He half gestured toward the gun and said, "What's that for?"

"A little trouble, bub," Melaven said mildly. "Come back for your money?"

"Yeah," Johnny said slowly.

Suddenly it came to him, and he wheeled and looked out through the broken window and saw Alec Barr across the street in conversation with two men, his own hands, Johnny supposed. That explained the shot that wakened him. A little trouble.

He looked back at Melaven now in time to hear him say to Cassie, "Give him his money."

Cassie came past him to the desk and pulled open a drawer and opened the cash box. While she was doing it, Johnny strolled soberly over to the desk. She gave him the dollar and he took it, and their glances met. She's been crying, he thought, with a strange distress.

"That's what I tried to tell you," Cassie said. "We didn't want to take your money, but you wouldn't have it. That's why I was so mean."

"What's it all about?" Johnny asked soberly.

"Didn't you read the paper?"

Johnny shook his head in negation, and Cassie said dully, "It's right there on page one. There's a big chunk of Government land out on Artillery Creek coming up for sale. Alec Barr wanted it, but he didn't want anybody bidding against him. He knew pa would have to publish a notice of sale. He tried to get pa to hold off publication of the date of sale until it would be too late for other bidders to make it. Pa was to get a piece of the land in return for the favor, or money. I guess we needed it all right, but pa told him no."

Johnny looked over at Melaven, who had come up to the rail now and was listening. Melaven said, "I knew Barr'd be in today with his bunch, and they'd want a look at a pull sheet before the press got busy, just to make sure the notice wasn't there. Well, Cassie and Dad Hopper worked with me all last night to turn out the real paper, with the notice of sale and a front-page editorial about Barr's proposition to me, to boot."

"We got it printed and hid it out in the shed early this morning," Cassie explained.

Melaven grinned faintly at Cassie, and there was a kind of open admiration for the job in the way he smiled. He said to Johnny now, "So what you saw in the forms this mornin' was a fake, bub. That's why Cassie didn't want your money. The paper was already printed." He smiled again, that rather proud smile. "After you'd gone, Barr came in. He wanted a pull sheet and we gave it to him, and he had a man out front watching us most of the morning. But he pulled him off later. We got the real paper out of the shed onto the Willow Valley stage, and we got it delivered all over town before Barr saw it."

Johnny was silent a moment, thinking this over. Then he nodded toward the window. "Barr do that?"

"I did," Melaven said quietly. "I reckon I can keep him out until someone in this town gets the guts to run him off."

Johnny looked down at the dollar in his hand and stared at it a moment and put it in his pocket. When he looked up at Cassie, he surprised her watching him, and she smiled a little, as if to ask forgiveness.

Johnny said, "Want any help?" to Melaven, and the man looked at him thoughtfully and then nodded. "Yes. You can take Cassie home."

"Oh, no," Cassie said. She backed away from the desk and put her back against the wall, looking from one to the other. "I don't go. As long as I'm here, he'll stay there."

"Sooner or later, he'll come in," Melaven said grimly. "I don't want you hurt."

"Let him come," Cassie said stubbornly. "I can swing a wrench better than some of his crew can shoot."

"Please go with him."

Cassie shook her head. "No, pa. There's some men left in this town. They'll turn up."

Melaven said "Hell," quietly, angrily, and went back into the shop. Johnny and the girl looked at each other for a long moment, and Johnny saw the fear in her eyes. She was fighting it, but she didn't have it licked, and he couldn't blame her. He said, "If I'd had a gun on me, I don't reckon they'd of let me in here, would they?"

"Don't try it again," Cassie said. "Don't try the back either. They're out there."

Johnny said, "Sure you won't come with me?"

"I'm sure."

"Good," Johnny said quietly. He stepped outside and turned upstreet, glancing over at Barr and the three men with him, who were watching him wordlessly. The man leaning against the building straightened up and asked, "She comin' out?"

"She's thinkin' it over," Johnny said.

The man called across the street to Barr, "She's thinkin' it over," and Johnny headed obliquely across the wide street toward the Elite. *What kind of a town is this, where they'd let this happen?* he thought angrily, and then he caught sight of Gus Irby standing under the wooden awning in front of the

Elite, watching the show. Everybody else was doing the same thing. A man behind Johnny yelled, "Send her out, Melaven," and Johnny vaulted up onto the boardwalk and halted in front of Gus.

"What do you aim to do?" he asked Gus.

"Mind my own business, same as you," Gus growled, but he couldn't hold Johnny's gaze.

There was shame in his face, and when Johnny saw it his mind was made up. He shouldered past him and went into the Elite and saw it was empty. He stepped behind the bar now and, bent over so he could look under it, slowly traveled down it. Right beside the beer taps he found what he was looking for. It was a sawed-off shotgun and he lifted it up and broke it and saw that both barrels were loaded. Standing motionless, he thought about this now, and presently he moved on toward the back and went out the rear door. It opened onto an alley, and he turned left and went up it, thinking, *It was brick, and the one next to it was painted brown, at least in front.* And then he saw it up ahead, a low brick store with a big loading platform running across its rear.

He went up to it, and looked down the narrow passageway he'd remembered was between this building and the brown one beside it. There was a small areaway here, this end cluttered with weeds and bottles and tin cans. Looking through it he could see a man's elbow and segment of leg at the boardwalk, and he stepped as noiselessly as he could over the trash and worked forward to the boardwalk.

At the end of the areaway, he hauled up and looked out and saw Alec Barr some ten feet to his right and teetering on the edge of the high boardwalk, gun in hand. He was engaged in low conversation with three other men on either side of him. There was a supreme insolence in the way he exposed himself, as if he knew Melaven would not shoot at him and could not hit him if he did.

Johnny raised the shotgun hip high and stepped out and said quietly, "Barr, you goin' to throw away that gun and get on your horse or am I goin' to burn you down?"

The four men turned slowly, not moving anything except their heads. It was Barr whom Johnny watched, and he saw the man's bold baleful eyes gauge his chances and decline the risk, and Johnny smiled. The three other men were watching Barr for a clue to their moves.

Johnny said "Now," and on the heel of it he heard the faint clatter of a kicked tin can in the areaway behind him. He lunged out of the areaway just as a pistol shot erupted with a savage roar between the two buildings.

Barr half turned now with the swiftness with which he lifted his gun across his front, and Johnny, watching him, didn't even raise the shotgun in his haste; he let go from the hip. He saw Barr rammed off the high board-walk into the tie rail, and heard it crack and splinter and break with the big man's weight, and then Barr fell in the street out of sight.

The three other men scattered into the street, running blindly for the op-posite sidewalk. And at the same time, the men who had been standing in front of the buildings watching this now ran toward Barr, and Gus Irby was in the van. Johnny poked the shotgun into the areaway and without even taking sight he pulled the trigger and listened to the bellow of the explosion and the rattling raking of the buckshot as it caromed between the two build-ings. Afterward, he turned down the street and let Gus and the others run past him, and he went into the Elite.

It was empty, and he put the shotgun on the bar and got himself a glass of water and stood there drinking it, thinking, *I feel some different, but not much.*

He was still drinking water when Gus came in later. Gus looked at him long and hard, as he poured himself a stout glass of whisky and downed it. Finally, Gus said, "There ain't a right thing about it, but they won't pay you a bounty for him. They should."

Johnny didn't say anything, only rinsed out his glass.

"Melaven wants to see you," Gus said then.

"All right." Johnny walked past him and Gus let him get past him ten feet, and then said, "Kid, look."

Johnny halted and turned around and Gus, looking sheepish, said, "About that there newspaper piece. That was meant to be a rawhide, but damned if it didn't backfire on me."

Johnny just waited, and Gus went on. "You remember the man that was standing this side of Barr? He works for me, runs some cows for me. Did, I mean, because he stood there all afternoon sickin' Barr on Melaven. You want his job? Forty a month, top hand."

"Sure," Johnny said promptly.

Gus smiled expansively and said, "Let's have a drink on it."

"Tomorrow," Johnny said. "I don't aim to get a reputation for drinkin' all day long."

Gus looked puzzled, and then laughed. "Reputation? Who with? Who knows—" His talk faded off, and then he said quietly, "Oh."

Johnny waited long enough to see if Gus would smile, and when Gus didn't, he went out. Gus didn't smile after he'd gone either.

The Defense of Freedom

In 1943, when Fred Glidden was writing "Top Hand," two things were certain: powers of unprecedented evil were out to dominate the free world, and its survival would depend upon the strength of its youth. The story appeared in the *Saturday Evening Post*, surrounded by ads showing clean-cut young American soldiers carrying rifles. Other ads showed the young women rolling up their sleeves to do the work needed on the home front.

Winston Churchill might well have been talking about young Johnny McSorley and Cassie Melaven when he said, "You will make all kind of mistakes; but as long as you are generous and true, and also fierce, you cannot hurt the world or even seriously distress her. She was made to be wooed and won by youth."

The world of these two resolute young people is somewhere in the West, a town called Wagon Mound. Glidden doesn't say so, but it could well be the little town of that name in New Mexico's northeast corner, ninety miles west of the dry-country of Texas. A cowhand drifting his way from Texas toward Arizona or Utah might stop in Wagon Mound before crossing the Sangre de Cristo range.

The story is a little vague about the location of Wagon Mound, but the conflict is clear-cut. Dan Melaven, owner and editor of the *Free Press*, stands squarely behind the ideals of democracy, fair play, and freedom of expression. Alec Barr, range tyrant and land grabber, openly practices intimidation, bribery, and dishonesty. The rest of the town is wavering, unwilling to risk Barr's wrath in order to support Melaven's idealism.

Young Johnny McSorley neither wavers nor hesitates. But what are his real motives? *That makes four times* he thinks when one more person calls him "son" or "bub" or "kid." Does he take up the gun in order to prove that he is more than just a kid? Is he trying to impress that "spitfire" Cassie Melaven? Or is his motive higher than these, an outraged sense of democracy and justice and a sure instinct for knowing what has to be done?

One motive, or several? In any case, Glidden spares us any unnecessary bragging and bravado. The gunfight, as quick and efficient as it is "fierce," shows what happens when a young American decides to defend freedom.

John M. Cunningham

b. 1915

John Cunningham, according to his own account, grew up in New York, New Jersey, California, and Virginia, and made a living in a variety of jobs, including tending store on a Montana dude ranch, clearing fire-breaks in California, picking grapes, and installing "a primitive IBM electronic bookkeeping system in a San Francisco bank."

During his college days in Virginia, Cunningham decided that he wanted to be a writer "because it was the only thing I was good at." And so after four years in the army, most of it in the South Pacific, the Philippines, and Japan, Cunningham began to write. His list of published works contains short stories (both western and non-western) and novels, including: *Warhorse: A Novel of the Old West* (1956) and *The Rainbow Runner* (1992).

Cunningham's best-known success is probably the story with which he first broke into the "slicks." He had sold stories to the pulp western magazines, like *Adventure*, *Dime Western*, and *Fifteen Western Tales*, but starting with "The Tin Star" his stories began to be published by higher-quality magazines like *Colliers*, *Redbook*, *Saturday Evening Post*, and *Cosmopolitan* (which used to publish western fiction on a fairly regular basis!).

"The Tin Star" has also made Cunningham's name familiar to fans of the western film, since screenwriter Carl Foreman used it as the basis for the script of *High Noon* (1952).

The Tin Star

Sheriff Doane looked at his deputy and then down at the daisies he had picked for his weekly visit, lying wrapped in newspaper on his desk. "I'm sorry to hear you say that, Toby. I was kind of counting on you to take over after me."

"Don't get me wrong, Doane," Toby said, looking through the front window. "I'm not afraid. I'll see you through this shindig. I'm not afraid of Jordan or young Jordan or any of them. But I want to tell you now. I'll wait till Jordan's train gets in. I'll wait to see what he does. I'll see you through whatever happens. After that, I'm quitting."

Doane began kneading his knuckles, his face set against the pain as he gently rubbed the misshapen, twisted bones. Using his fists all these years hadn't helped the gout. He said nothing.

Toby looked around, his brown eyes troubled in his round, olive-skinned face. "What's the use of holding down a job like this? Look at you. What'd you ever get of it? Enough to keep you eating. And what for?"

Doane stopped kneading his arthritic hands and looked down at the star on his shirt front. He looked from it to the smaller one on Toby's. "That's right," he said. "They don't even hang the right ones. You risk your life catching somebody, and the damned juries let them go so they can come back and shoot at you. You're poor all your life, you got to do everything twice, and in the end they pay you off in lead. So you can wear a tin star. It's a job for a dog, son."

Toby's voice did not rise, but his eyes were a little wider in his round, gentle face. "Then why keep on with it? What for? I been working for you for two years—trying to keep the law so sharp-nosed money-grabbers can get rich, while we piddle along on what the county pays us. I've seen men I used to bust playing marbles going up and down this street on four-hundred dollar saddles, and what've I got? Nothing. Not a damned thing."

There was a little smile around Doane's wide mouth. "That's right, Toby.

It's all for free. The headaches, the bullets and everything, all for free. I found that out long ago." The mock-grave look vanished. "But somebody's got to be around and take care of things." He looked out of the window at the people walking up and down the crazy boardwalks. "I like it free. You know what I mean? You don't get a thing for it. You've got to risk everything. And you're free inside. Like the larks. You know the larks? How they get up in the sky and sing when they want to? A pretty bird. A very pretty bird. That's the way I like to feel inside."

Toby looked at him without expression. "That's the way you look at it. I don't see it. I've only got one life. You talk about doing it all for nothing, and that gives you something. What? What've you got now, waiting for Jordan to come?"

"I don't know yet. We'll have to wait and see."

Toby turned back to the window. "All right, but I'm through. I don't see any sense in risking your neck for nothing."

"Maybe you will," Doane said, beginning to work on his hands again.

"Here comes Mettrick. I guess he don't give up so easy. He's still got that resignation in his hand."

"I guess he doesn't," Doane said. "But I'm through listening. Has young Jordan come out of the saloon yet?"

"No," Toby said, and stepped aside as the door opened. Mettrick came in. "Now listen, Doane," he burst out, "for the last time—"

"Shut up, Percy," Doane said. "Sit down over there and shut up or get out."

The flare went out of the mayor's eyes. "Doane," he moaned, "you are the biggest—"

"Shut up," Doane said. "Toby, has he come out yet?"

Toby stood a little back from the window, where the slant of golden sunlight, swarming with dust, wouldn't strike his white shirt.

"Yes. He's got a chair. He's looking this way, Doane. He's still drinking. I can see a bottle on the porch beside him."

"I expected that. Not that it makes much difference." He looked down at the bunch of flowers.

Mettrick, in the straight chair against the wall, looked up at him, his black eyes scornful in his long, hopeless face.

"Don't make much difference? Who the hell do you think you are, Doane? God? It just means he'll start the trouble without waiting for his stinking brother, that's all it means." His hand was shaking, and the white paper hanging listlessly from his fingers fluttered slightly. He looked at it angrily and stuck it out at Doane. "I gave it to you. I did the best I could. Whatever happens, don't be blaming me, Doane. I gave you a chance to resign, and if—" He left off and sat looking at the paper in his hand as though it were a dead puppy of his that somebody had run a buggy over.

Doane standing with the square almost chisel-pointed tips of his fingers just touching the flowers, turned slowly with the care of movement he would have used around a crazy horse. "I know you're my friend, Percy. Just take it easy, Percy. If I don't resign, it's not because I'm ungrateful."

"Here comes Staley with the news," Toby said from the window. "He looks like somebody just shot his grandma."

Percy Mettrick laid his paper on the desk, and began smoothing it out carefully. "It's not as though it were dishonorable, Doane. You should have quit two years ago, when your hands went bad. It's not dishonorable now. You've still got time."

He glanced up at the wall clock. "It's only three. You've got an hour before it gets in, you can take your horse . . ." As he talked to himself, Doane looked slantwise at him with his little smile. He grew more cheerful. "Here." He jabbed a pen out at Doane. "Sign it and get out of town."

The smile left Doane's mouth. "This is an elective office. I don't have to take orders, even if you are mayor." His face softened. "It's simpler than you think, Percy. When they didn't hang Jordan, I knew this day would come. Five years ago, I knew it was coming, when they gave him that silly sentence. I've been waiting for it."

"But not to commit suicide," Mettrick said in a low voice, his eyes going down to Doane's gouty hands. Doane's knobby, twisted fingers closed slowly into fists, as though hiding themselves; his face flushed slightly. "I may be slow, but I can still shoot."

The mayor stood up and went slowly over to the door.

"Goodbye, Doane."

"I'm not saying goodbye, Percy. Not yet."

"Goodbye," Mettrick repeated. He went out of the door.

Toby turned from the window. His face was tight around the mouth. "You should have resigned like he said, Doane. You ain't a match for one of them, much less two of them together. And if Pierce and Frank Colby come, too, like they was all together before—"

"Shut up, shut up," Doane said. "For God's sake, shut up." He sat down suddenly at the desk and covered his face with his hands. "Maybe the pen changes a man." He was sitting stiff, hardly breathing.

"What are you going to do, Doane?"

"Nothing. I can't do anything until they start something. I can't do a thing. . . . Maybe the pen changes a man. Sometimes it does. I remember—"

"Listen, Doane," Toby said, his voice, for the first time, urgent. "It maybe changes some men, but not Jordan. It's already planned, what they're going to do. Why else would young Jordan be over there, watching? He's come three hundred miles for this."

"I've seem men go in the pen hard as rock and come out peaceful and settle down. Maybe Jordan—"

Toby's face relapsed into dullness. He turned back to the window listlessly. Doane's hands dropped.

"You don't think that's true, Toby?"

Toby sighed. "You know it isn't so, Doane. He swore he'd get you. That's the truth."

Doane's hands came up again in front of his face, but this time he was looking at them, his big gray eyes going quickly from one to the other, almost as though he were afraid of them. He curled his fingers slowly into fists, and uncurled them slowly, pulling with all his might, yet slowly. A thin sheen on his face reflected the sunlight from the floor. He got up.

"Is he still there?" he asked.

"Sure, he's still there."

"Maybe he'll get drunk. Dead drunk."

"You can't get a Jordan that drunk."

Doane stood with feet apart, looking at the floor, staring back and forth along one of the cracks. "Why didn't they hang him?" he asked the silence in the room.

"Why didn't they hang him?" he repeated, his voice louder.

Toby kept his post by the window, not moving a muscle in his face, staring out at the man across the street. "I don't know," he said. "For murder, they should, I guess they should, but they didn't."

Doane's eyes came again to the flowers, and some of the strain went out of his face. Then suddenly his eyes closed and he gave a long sigh, and then, luxuriously, stretched his arms. "Good God!" he said, his voice easy again. "It's funny how it comes over you like that." He shook his head violently. "I don't know why it should. It's not the first time. But it always does."

"I know," Toby said.

"It just builds up and then it busts."

"I know."

"The train may be late."

Toby said nothing.

"You never can tell," Doane said, buckling on his gun belt. "Things may have changed with Jordan. Maybe he won't even come. You never can tell. I'm going up to the cemetery as soon as we hear from Staley."

"I wouldn't. You'd just tempt young Jordan to start something."

"I've been going up there every Sunday since she died."

"We'd best both just stay in here. Let them make the first move."

Feet sounded on the steps outside and Doane stopped breathing for a second. Staley came in, his face pinched, tight and dead, his eyes on the floor. Doane looked him over carefully.

"Is it on time?" he asked steadily.

Staley looked up, his faded blue eyes, distant, pointed somewhere over Doane's head. "Mr. Doane, you ain't handled this thing right. You should of drove young Jordan out of town." His hand went to his chest and he took off the deputy's badge.

"What are you doing?" Doane asked sharply.

"If you'd of handled it right, we could have beat this," Staley said, his voice louder.

"You know nobody's done nothing yet," Toby said softly, his gentle brown eyes on Staley. "There's nothing we can do until they start something."

"I'm quitting, Mr. Doane," Staley said. He looked around for someplace to put the star. He started for the desk, hesitated, and then awkwardly, with a peculiar diffidence, laid the star gently on the window sill.

Doane's jaw began to jut a little. "You still haven't answered my question. Is the train on time?"

"Yes. Four ten. Just on time." Staley stood staring at Doane, then swallowed. "I saw Frank Colby. He was in the livery putting up his horse. He'd had a long ride on that horse. I asked him what he was doing in town—friendly like." He ducked his head and swallowed again. "He didn't know I was a deputy. I had my star off." He looked up again. "They're all meeting together, Mr. Doane. Young Jordan, and Colby and Pierce. They're going to meet Jordan when he comes in. The same four."

"So you're quitting," Doane said.

"Yes, sir. It ain't been handled right."

Toby stood looking at him, his gentle eyes dull. "Get out," he said, his voice low and tight.

Staley looked at him, nodded and tried to smile, which was too weak to last. "Sure."

Toby took a step toward him. Staley's eyes were wild as he stood against the door. He tried to back out of Toby's way.

"Get out," Toby said again, and his small brown fist flashed out. Staley stepped backward and fell down the steps in a sprawling heap, scrambled to his feet and hobbled away. Toby closed the door slowly. He stood rubbing his knuckles, his face red and tight.

"That didn't do any good," Doane said softly.

Toby turned on him. "It couldn't do no harm," he said acidly, throwing the words into Doane's face.

"You want to quit, too?" Doane asked, smiling.

"Sure, I want to quit," Toby shot out. "Sure. Go on to your blasted cemetery, go on with your flowers, old man—" He sat down suddenly on the straight chair. "Put a flower up there for me, too."

Doane went to the door. "Put some water on the heater, Toby. Set out the liniment that the vet gave me. I'll try it again when I get back. It might do some good yet."

Then he let himself out and stood in the sunlight on the porch, the flowers drooping in his hand, looking against the sun across the street at the dim figure under the shaded porch.

Then he saw the two other shapes hunkered against the front of the saloon in the shade of the porch, one on each side of young Jordan, who sat tilted back in a chair. Colby and Pierce. The glare of the sun beat back from the blinding white dust and fought shimmering in the air.

Doane pulled the brim of his hat farther down in front and stepped slowly down to the board sidewalk, observing just as carefully, avoiding any pause which might be interpreted as a challenge.

Young Jordan had the bottle to his lips as Doane came out. He held it there for a moment motionless, and then, as Doane reached the walk, he passed the bottle slowly sideward to Colby and leaned forward, away from the wall, so that the chair came down softly. He sat there, leaning forward slightly, watching while Doane untied his horse. As Doane mounted, Jordan got up. Colby's hand grabbed one of his arms. He shook it off and untied his own horse from the rail.

Doane's mouth tightened and his eyes looked a little sad. He turned his horse, and holding the flowers so the jog would not rattle off the petals, headed up the street, looking straight ahead.

The hoofs of his horse made soft, almost inaudible little plops in the deep dust. Behind him he heard a sudden stamping of hoofs and then the harsh splitting and crash of wood. He looked back. Young Jordan's horse was up on the sidewalk, wild-eyed and snorting with young Jordan leaning forward half out of the saddle, pushing himself back from the horse's neck, back off the horn into the saddle, swaying insecurely. And as Jordan managed the horse off the sidewalk Doane looked quickly forward again, his eyes fixed distantly ahead and blank.

He passed men he knew, and out of the corner of his eye he saw their glances slowly follow him, calm, or gloomy, or shrewdly speculative. As he passed, he knew their glances were shifting to the man whose horse was softly coming up behind him. It was like that all the way up the street. The flowers were drooping markedly now.

The town petered out with a few Mexican shacks, the road dwindled to broad ruts, and the sage was suddenly on all sides of him, stretching away toward the heat-obscured mountains like an infinite multitude of gray-green sheep. He turned off the road and began the slight ascent up the little hill whereon the cemetery lay. Grasshoppers thrilled invisibly in the sparse, dried grass along the track, silent as he came by, and shrill again as he passed, only to become silent again as the other rider came.

He swung off at the rusty barbed wire Missouri gate and slipped the loop from the post, and the shadow of the other slid tall across his path and stopped. Doane licked his lips quickly and looked up, his grasp tightening on the now sweat-wilted newspaper. Young Jordan was sitting his horse, open-mouthed, leaning forward with his hands on the pommel to support himself, his eyes vague and dull. His lips were wet and red, and hung in a slight smile.

A lark made the air sweet over to the left, and then Doane saw it, rising into the air. It hung in the sun, over the cemetery. Moving steadily and avoiding all suddenness, Doane hung his reins over the post.

"You don't like me, do you?" young Jordan said. A long thread of saliva descended from the corner of his slackly smiling mouth.

Doane's face set into a sort of blank preparedness. He turned and started slowly through the gate, his shoulders hunched up and pulled backward.

Jordan got down from the saddle, and Doane turned toward him slowly. Jordan came forward straight enough, with his feet apart, braced against staggering. He stopped three feet from Doane, bent forward, his mouth slightly open.

"You got any objections to me being in town?"

"No," Doane said, and stood still.

Jordan thought that over, his eyes drifting idly sideways for a moment. Then they came back, to a finer focus this time, and he said, "Why not?"

hunching forward again, his hands open and held away from the holsters at his hips.

Doane looked at the point of his nose. "You haven't done anything, Jordan. Except get drunk. Nothing to break the law."

"I haven't done nothing," Jordan said, his eyes squinting away at one of the small, tilting tombstones. "By God, I'll do something. Whadda I got to do?" He drew his head back, as though he were farsighted, and squinted. "Whadda I got to do to make you fight, huh?"

"Don't do anything," Doane said quietly, keeping his voice even. "Just go back and have another drink. Have a good time."

"You think I ain't sober enough to fight?" Jordan slipped his right gun out of its holster, turning away from Doane. Doane stiffened. "Wait, mister," Jordan said.

He cocked the gun. "See that bird?" He raised the gun into the air, squinting along the barrel. The bright nickel of its finish gleamed in the sun. The lark wheeled and fluttered. Jordan's arm swung unsteadily in a small circle.

He pulled the trigger and the gun blasted. The lark jumped in the air, flew away about twenty feet, and began circling again, catching insects.

"Missed 'im," Jordan mumbled, lowering his arm and wiping sweat off his forehead. "Damn it, I can't see!" He raised his arm again. Again the heavy blast cracked Doane's ears. Down in the town, near the Mexican huts, he could see tiny figures run out into the street.

The bird didn't jump this time, but darted away out of sight over the hill.

"Got him," Jordan said, scanning the sky. His eyes wandered over the graveyard for a moment, looking for the bird's body. "Now you see?" he said, turning to Doane, his eyes blurred and watering with the sun's glare. "I'm going down and shoot up the damned town. Come down and stop me, you old—"

He turned and lurched sideways a step, straightened himself out and walked more steadily toward his horse, laughing to himself. Doane turned away, his face sick, and trudged slowly up the hill, his eye on the ground.

He stopped at one of the newer graves. The headstone was straight on this one. He looked at it, his face changing expression. "Here lies Cecelia Doane, born 1837, died 1885, the loyal wife . . ."

He stopped and pulled a weed from the side of the grave, then pulled a bunch of withered stems from a small green funnel by the headstone, and awkwardly took the fresh flowers out of the newspaper. He put the flowers into the funnel, wedging them firmly down into the bottom, and set it down again. He stood up and moved back, wiping sweat from his eyes.

A sudden shout came from the gate, and the sharp crack of a quirt. Doane turned with a befuddled look.

Jordan was back on his horse, beating Doane's. He had looped the reins over its neck so that it would run free. It was tearing away down the slope headed back for town.

Doane stood with his hat in his hand, his face suddenly beet red. He took a step after Jordan, and then stood still, shaking a little. He stared fixedly after him, watching him turn into the main road and toward the main street again. Then, sighing deeply, he turned back to the grave. Folding the newspaper, he began dusting off the heavy slab, whispering to himself. "No, Cissie, I could have gone. But, you know—it's my town."

He straightened up, his face flushed, put on his hat, and slapping the folded paper against his knee, started down the path. He got to the Missouri gate, closed it, and started down the ruts again.

A shot came from the town, and he stopped. Then there were two more, sharp spurts of sound coming clear and definite across the sage. He made out a tiny figure in a blue shirt running along a sidewalk.

He stood stock-still, the grasshoppers singing in a contented chorus all around him in the bright yellow glare. A train whistle came faint from off the plain, and he looked far across it. He made out the tiny trailed plume of smoke.

His knees began to quiver very slightly and he began to walk, very slowly, down the road.

Then suddenly there came a splatter of shots from below. The train whistle came again, louder, a crying wail of despair in the burning, brilliant, dancing air.

He began to hurry, stumbling a little in the ruts. And then he stopped short, his face open in fear. "My God, my empty horse, those shots—Toby, no!" He began to run, shambling, awkward and stumbling, his face ashen.

From the end of the street, as he hobbled panting past the tight-shut Mexican shanties, he could see a blue patch in the dust in front of the saloon, and shambled to a halt. It wasn't Toby, whoever it was, lying there face down: face buried in the deep, pillowing dust, feet still on the board sidewalk where the man had been standing.

The street was empty. None of the faces he knew looked at him now. He drew one of his guns and cocked it and walked fast up the walk, on the saloon side.

A shot smashed ahead of him and he stopped, shrinking against a store front. Inside, through the glass door, he could see two pale faces in the murk. Blue powder smoke curled out from under the saloon porch ahead of him.

Another shot smashed, this time from his office. The spurt of smoke, almost invisible in the sunlight, was low down in the doorway. Two horses were loose in the street now, his own, standing alert up past the saloon, and young Jordan's half up on the boardwalk under one of the porches.

He walked forward, past young Jordan's horse, to the corner of the saloon building. Another shot slammed out of his office door, the bullet smacking the window ahead of him. A small, slow smile grew on his mouth. He looked sideways at the body in the street. Young Jordan lay with the back of his head open to the sun, crimson and brilliant, his bright nickel gun still in his right hand, its hammer still cocked, unfired.

The train whistle moaned again, closer.

"Doane," Toby called from the office door, invisible. "Get out of town." There was a surge of effort in the voice, a strain that made it almost a squeal. "I'm shot in the leg. Get out before they get together."

A door slammed somewhere. Doane glanced down between the saloon and the store beside it. Then he saw, fifty yards down the street, a figure come out of another side alley and hurry away down the walk toward the station. From the saloon door another shot slammed across the street. Toby held his fire.

Doane peered after the running figure, his eyes squinting thoughtfully. The train's whistle shrieked again like the ultimatum of an approaching conqueror at the edge of town, and in a moment the ground under his feet began to vibrate slightly and the hoarse roar of braking wheels came up the street.

He turned back to young Jordan's horse, petted it around the head a moment and then took it by the reins close to the bit. He guided it across the street, keeping its body between him and the front of the saloon, without drawing fire, and went on down the alley beside his office. At the rear door he hitched the horse and went inside.

Toby was on the floor, a gun in his hand, his hat beside him, peering out across the sill. Doane kept low, beneath the level of the window, and crawled up to him. Toby's leg was twisted peculiarly and blood leaked steadily out from the boot top onto the floor. His face was sweating and very pale, and his lips were tight. "I thought he got you," Toby said keeping his eyes on the saloon across the street. "I heard those shots and then your horse came bucketing back down the street. I got Jordan. Colby got me in the leg before I got back inside."

"Never mind about that. Come on, get on your feet if you can and I'll help you on the horse in back. You can get out of town and I'll shift for myself."

"I think I'm going to pass out. I don't want to move. It won't hurt no worse getting killed than it does now. The hell with the horse! Take it yourself."

Doane looked across the street, his eyes moving over the door and the windows carefully, inch by inch.

"I'm sorry I shot him," Toby said. "It's my fault. And it's my fight now, Doane. Clear out."

Doane turned and scuttled out of the back. He mounted the horse and rode down behind four stores. He turned up another alley, dashed across the main street, down another alley, then back up behind the saloon.

He dismounted, his gun cocked in his hand. The back door of the place was open and he got through it quickly, the sound of his boot heels dimmed under the blast of a shot from the front of the saloon. From the dark rear of the room, he could see Pierce, crouched behind the bar, squinting through a bullet hole in the stained-glass bottom half of the front window.

There was a bottle of whisky standing on the bar beside Pierce; he reached out a hand and tilted the bottle up to his mouth, half turning toward Doane as he did so. Pierce kept the bottle to his lips, pretending to drink, and, with his right hand invisible behind the bar, brought his gun into line with Doane.

The tip of Pierce's gun came over the edge of the bar, the rest of him not moving a hair and Doane, gritting his teeth, squeezed slowly and painfully on his gun trigger. The gun flamed and bucked in his hand, and he dropped it, his face twisting in agony. The bottle fell out of Pierce's hand and spun slowly on the bar. Pierce sat there for a moment before his head fell forward and he crashed against the edge of the bar and slipped down out of sight.

Doane picked up his gun with his left hand and walked forward to the bar, holding his right hand like a crippled paw in front of him. The bottle had stopped revolving. Whisky inside it, moving back and forth, rocked it gently. He righted it and took a short pull at the neck, and in a moment the pain lines relaxed in his face. He went to the bat-wing doors and pushed one of them partly open.

"Toby!" he called.

There was no answer from across the street, and then he saw the barrel of a revolver sticking out of his office door, lying flat, and behind it one hand, curled loosely and uselessly around the butt.

He looked down the street. The train stood across it. A brakeman moved along the cars slowly, his head down. There was nobody else in sight.

He started to step out, and saw then two men coming up the opposite walk, running fast. Suddenly one of them stopped, grabbing the other by the arm, and pointed at him. He stared back for a moment, seeing Jordan clearly now, the square, hard face unchanged except for its pallor, bleak and bony as before.

Doane let the door swing to and continued to watch them over the top of it. They talked for a moment. Then Colby ran back down the street—well out of effective range—sprinted across it and disappeared. Down the street the engine, hidden by some building, chuffed angrily, and the cars began to move again. Jordan stood still, leaning against the front of a building, fully exposed, a hard smile on his face.

Doane turned and hurried to the back door. It opened outward. He slammed and bolted it, then hurried back to the front and waited, his gun ready. He smiled as the back door rattled, turned, fired a shot at it and listened. For a moment there was no sound. Then something solid hit it, bumped a couple of times and silence came again.

From the side of the building, just beyond the corner where Pierce's body lay, a shot crashed. The gun in the office door jumped out of the hand and spun wildly. The hand lay still.

He heard Jordan's voice from down the street, calling, the words formed slowly, slightly spaced.

"Is he dead?"

"Passed out," Colby called back.

"I'm going around back to get him. Keep Doane inside." Jordan turned and disappeared down an alley.

Doane leaned across the bar, knocked bottles off the shelves of the back bar and held his pistol on the corner of the wall, about a foot above the floor.

"Pierce," he said.

"Throw out your guns," Pierce answered.

Doane squinted at the corner, moved his gun slightly and fired. He heard a cry of pain, then curses; saw the bat-wing doors swing slightly. Then he turned and ran for the back door. He threw back the bolt and pushed on the door. It wouldn't give. He threw himself against it. It gave a little at the bottom. Colby had thrown a stake up against it to keep him locked in.

He ran back to the front.

Across the street, he could see somebody moving in his office, dimly, beyond the window. Suddenly the hand on the floor disappeared.

"Come on out, you old—" Pierce said, panting. "You only skinned me." His voice was closer than before, somewhere between the door and the corner of the building, below the level of the stained glass.

Then Doane saw Toby's white shirt beyond the window opposite. Jordan was holding him up, and moving toward the door. Jordan came out on the porch, hugging Toby around the chest, protecting himself with the limp body. With a heave he sent Toby flying down the steps, and jumped back out of sight. Toby rolled across the sidewalk and fell into the street, where he lay motionless.

Doane looked stupidly at Toby, then at young Jordan, still lying with his feet cocked up on the sidewalk.

"He ain't dead, Doane," Jordan called. "Come and get him if you want him alive." He fired through the window. Dust jumped six inches from Toby's head. "Come on out, Doane, and shoot it out. You got a chance to save him." The gun roared again, and dust jumped a second time beside Toby's head, almost in the same spot.

"Leave the kid alone," Doane called. "This fight's between you and me."

"The next shot kills him, Doane."

Doane's face sagged white and he leaned against the side of the door. He could hear Pierce breathing heavily in the silence, just outside. He pushed himself away from the door and drew a breath through clenched teeth. He cocked his pistol and strode out, swinging around. Pierce fired from the sidewalk, and Doane aimed straight into the blast and pulled as he felt himself flung violently around by Pierce's bullet.

Pierce came up from the sidewalk and took two steps toward him, opening and shutting a mouth that was suddenly full of blood, his eyes wide and wild, and then pitched down at his feet.

Doane's right arm hung useless, his gun at his feet. With his left hand he drew his other gun and stepped out from the walk, his mouth wide open, as though he were gasping for breath or were about to scream, and took two steps toward Toby as Jordan came out of the office door, firing. The slug caught Doane along the side of his neck, cutting his shoulder muscle, and his head fell over to one side. He staggered on, firing. He saw Toby trying to get up, saw Jordan fall back against the building, red running down the front of his shirt, and the smile gone.

Jordan stood braced against the building, holding his gun in both hands, firing as he slid slowly down. One bullet took Doane in the stomach, another in the knee. He went down, flopped forward and dragged himself up to where Toby lay trying to prop himself up on one elbow. Doane knelt there like a dog, puking blood into the dust, blood running out of his nose, but his gray eyes almost indifferent, as though there were one man dying and another watching.

He saw Jordan lift his gun with both hands and aim it toward Toby, and as the hammer fell, he threw himself across Toby's head and took it in the back. He rolled off onto his back and lay staring into the sky.

Upside down, he saw Toby take his gun and get up on one elbow, level it at Jordan and fire, and then saw Toby's face, over his, looking down at him as the deputy knelt in the street.

They stayed that way for a long moment, while Doane's eyes grew more and more dull and the dark of his blood in the white dust grew broader. His breath was coming hard, in small sharp gasps.

"There's nothing in it, kid," he whispered. "Only a tin star. They don't hang the right ones. You got to fight everything twice. It's a job for a dog."

"Thank you, Doane."

"It's all for free. You going to quit, Toby?"

Toby looked down at the gray face, the mouth and chin and neck crimson, the grey eyes dull. Toby shook his head. His face was hard as a rock.

Doane's face suddenly looked a little surprised, his eyes went past Toby to the sky. Toby looked up. A lark was high above them, circling and fluttering, directly overhead. "A pretty bird," Doane mumbled. "A very pretty bird."

His head turned slowly to one side, and Toby looked down at him and saw him as though fast asleep.

He took Doane's gun in his hand, and took off Doane's star, and sat there in the street while men slowly came out of stores and circled about them. He sat there unmoving, looking at Doane's half-averted face, holding the two things tightly, one in each hand, like a child with a broken toy, his face soft and blurred, his eyes unwet.

After a while the lark went away. He looked up at the men, and saw Mettrick.

"I told him he should have resigned," Mettrick said, his voice high. "He could have taken his horse—"

"Shut up," Toby said. "Shut up or get out." His eyes were sharp and his face placid and set. He turned to another of the men. "Get the doc," he said. "I've got a busted leg. And I've got a lot to do."

The man looked at him, a little startled, and then ran.

The Privilege behind the Badge

Sometimes it is shaped like a star, sometimes like a shield. Some are stamped with the name of a town, and others with the name of a county, state, or nation. But whatever shape it has and whatever is stamped upon it, a badge always signifies the same thing: the person who carries it has the duty—and privilege—of executing the law. And the person is sworn to defend that bit of metal and what it stands for, if necessary with lethal force.

When feudalism held sway in medieval Europe, men of the upper classes were entitled to carry shields of their own design. The shield was a mark of privilege, but the privilege included an obligation to protect the lower classes from other nobles and men-at-arms. Feudalism gradually faded out, and the invention of firearms made shields and armor obsolete. However, today we still use a symbolic version of the shield as a badge of office and duty.

In this story of an early western town, Toby sees the badge only as a "tin star," and all he can think about, at first, is what it means in terms of money. Why, in the end, does he change his mind? Is it because he started the gunfight, in the belief that his friend Doane had been killed? Does he decide to become a lawman because he is outraged? Or is it that being wounded gives him a personal stake in the matter, which he did not have before?

None of these reasons is really strong enough. The real reason is simpler than that: Toby is a man who has been born to the badge. He is one of those rare individuals whose integrity, courage, and sense of duty entitle them to carry it. Like Doane, and like the medieval European knights, he has the privilege of fighting for the sake of law and order. Jordan violates the code: therefore, Doane and Toby have the task of engaging him in combat.

Several critics scoffed at the movie version of this story, *High Noon*. It was ridiculous, they said, to think of a whole town of tough frontier citizens hiding in their houses just because a few common lawbreakers had come to town. A real western town would greet Jordan's gang with Winchester rifles or shotguns sticking out of every doorway.

These critics missed the point. The moviemakers also missed the point: they used the sheriff's wife as the focal point of the suspense. Most of the tension in *High Noon* comes from her frustration: she is unable to understand how her man can face another man in a gunfight to the death.

But the woman is not important to the real point of Cunningham's story (which is probably why Cunningham makes Sheriff Doane a widower). The townspeople are not important, either. They are only the backdrop of the drama.

Think of the King Arthur tradition in which a knight is chosen to fight against evil in the kingdom. Perhaps a maiden or her aged father is being held hostage. That, however, does not matter as much as the fact that certain knights are born with integrity, courage, and a sense of duty. They have the privilege and the responsibility to uphold the peace of the land.

If those critics of *High Noon* had it their way, in the King Arthur stories it would be the ordinary townspeople who slay the dragon or end the siege or storm the castle or lynch the Black Prince. It might make an exciting battle, but it wouldn't tell us anything about individual duty and courage.

To get back to the basic question here, why *does* Toby stay? The sheriff says that it is like the bird, the lark that young Jordan tries to kill: "You've got to risk everything," Doane says, "and then you're free inside. Like the larks." However, that gift of the soaring spirit, that privilege of freedom, comes with a price on it. A *chevalier* of medieval France could tell us why Toby stays on as sheriff. "Noblesse oblige," the knight would say: nobility obligates.

Lewis B. Patten

1915–1981

Lewis Patten joined the navy when he was eighteen and served four years before returning to his native Denver. For the next three or four years he attended the University of Denver and worked as a senior auditor for the Colorado Department of Revenue. Then in 1943 he made a break with the city and went to operate a ranch across the Rockies in the mesa country of western Colorado.

So far, this does not sound like the background of a fiction writer, especially a writer who won a hatful of writing awards, published more than a hundred books, and had his work turned into television scripts and movies. But three years after taking up ranching, Lewis Patten also began writing. He published an average of three books per year until his death in 1981. And that doesn't include his short stories and television scripts.

Some of Patten's titles include *Gunsmoke Empire* (1955), *Cheyenne Drums* (1968), *Ride a Tall Horse* (1980), and *Vengeance Rider* (1983). His film credits include *Red Sundown* (Universal, 1956) and *Death of a Gunfighter* (Universal, 1969). The Western Writers of America presented him with their Golden Spur Award in 1969, 1970, and 1973 and the Golden Saddleman Award in 1979.

Massacre at Cottonwood Springs

The dust and the smell of the trail herds waiting outside of town came in on the small, hot, Kansas breeze. It made the percentage girls wrinkle their powdered noses distastefully, but it was not unpleasant to Russ Webber's nostrils. He sat, thin and ragged, on the high seat of the Conestoga wagon with his pa. The horses plodded ahead of the creaking wagon toward the center of town, and neither man nor boy saw or understood the trouble that was shaping up in front of the Mogollon Dance Palace.

Had Russ' pa been used to this sort of thing, he would have noticed the way men flattened themselves against the walls of the rough, unpainted buildings, the way the group of five stood tensely alone in front of the Mogollon. He might have noticed the man across the street and the bright star that gleamed from his vest.

Russ' ma poked her head up behind them, holding the baby. She said softly and with a sort of glad relief, "This is a good place, Mark. Let's stay here."

Russ remembered now the way pa had been getting down from the wagon the last two days, sifting the soil between his bony, rough, farmer's hands. He thought of the way pa's weathered face had softened, the way the keen blue eyes had kindled. So it was no surprise when pa said, "Sure, Nellie. This is a good spot. We'll take up a place an' put down our roots. It's time."

Their progress along the street was slow, but so was the thing slow in building to a climax in front of the Mogollon. There was a campground in the grove of cottonwoods on the other side of town, and it was toward this that they were heading.

Russ saw a woman poke her head out of the store next to the Mogollon and duck back hastily, and he wondered at her sudden, startled expression that looked like fear.

All motion in this wide, dusty street seemed suspended but that of the nester's wagon, and all sound was stilled but that of its creaking wheels.

They drew abreast of the Mogollon. The stillness of the men there ceased. They moved, and these movements had the quickness of light. There was a short flurry of motion on the other side of the wagon as the lone man there headed for a doorway. Russ caught a glint of sunlight on the bit of bright metal that adorned his vest.

This was a thing that Russ could not understand, but a thing that brought fear from some deep part of him. He looked at pa's face, seeking reassurance there, but saw only pa's panicked realization that they had blundered into a crossfire. The guns appeared in the hands of the men standing in front of the Mogollon. The marshal across the street was a mere blur of motion. Pa's rough hand laid itself on Russ' back and sprawled the boy on the floorboards. One of the group of five yelled, "The marshal's gittin' away! Shoot, damn you, shoot!"

The guns belched smoke straight at the nester's wagon, seeking the man now hidden from sight behind it, and bullets tore through the wagon as it moved into their path.

There was the sound of a solid, meaty smack beside Russ and above him. Pa fell forward, dropping the reins, falling between the horses. Ma screamed. Russ lay staring stupidly, no color in his white face, his eyes wide with this quick fear.

The silence was shocking. The team nervously danced, but life, except for Russ', had ceased in the wagon.

A man stepped into the street and caught at the bridle of the near horse, just as the frightened animals surged into a run. Pa's still form lay in the dusty street. Rifle fire now boomed, and in quick succession three of the gunmen in front of the Mogollon crumpled lifeless close by. The remaining two, their guns still smoking in their hands, broke into a ragged run. The rifle spoke again, and one of these stumbled and went down. The other rounded the corner beside Halliday's feed store and disappeared. The marshall stepped into the street from the doorway into which he had ducked, and crossed in the hushed silence that lay heavy and solid over this raw scene of death. He raged impotently, "Damn it, Dude got away!"

The street began to fill. Men poured from doorways all along the street. There was the sudden babble of excited talk. The marshal stirred the still figures on the board sidewalk with the toe of his boot, rifle held ready. A crowd formed around the tall Conestoga wagon, and a man peering in behind cried out, "God! They got the woman . . . an' the kid!"

Another breathed, "Five men, a woman, an' a kid. Oh, Lord!"

Russ sat shocked and still on the seat. He thought wonderingly, still failing to comprehend, "A minute ago, it was all so quiet. It was all so quiet."

Folks said it was kind of funny to see the darkly handsome, powerful marshal, Jeff Thomas, walking along the street with ragged, skinny Russ Webber tailing him. They said Jeff felt guilty on account of the way the kid's folks had died. They allowed that Jeff owed the boy something, because if it hadn't been for that nester's wagon, Jeff Thomas would have been a long time dead and the town of Cottonwood Springs looking for a new marshal.

Still, nobody blamed Jeff Thomas for what had happened. He'd tried to avoid gunfire by ducking out of sight in that doorway. He'd just been a little too late.

Folks thought fourteen-year-old Russ Webber a mite queer. The boy was sullen, looking at man and woman alike out of brooding, hate-filled eyes. He slouched after Jeff Thomas like a mangy dog, its tail tucked between its legs. He got to be a kind of a fixture around Cottonwood Springs that winter, and eventually the town got used to him, accepted him much as they accepted the everlasting mud in the street, the cold bite of the norther.

In April, as the marshal and the skinny, shivering boy rode through the thin slush of snow north of town, Russ asked, "Jeff, will Dude Sudler be comin' back here from Texas soon?"

For the hundredth time, Jeff answered wearily, "Reckon he will, boy. But you ain't ready for him yet. You got to practice more. You got to git faster. Dude Sudler is as mean as they come. He's fast as a sidewinder. You better let me take care of him."

They reached a spot where a wide, dry wash cut its ragged gash across the plain, and here they dismounted. Russ walked jerkily to the bank and, drawing from somewhere among his ragged garments, fired three quick shots at three white pebbles in the bank. Dust flew. He fired twice more. Two more pebbles disappeared. Jeff drawled, "You shoot mighty straight, kid, but you don't draw fast enough. If you'd let me buy you a holster . . ."

The boy shook his head, thinking of the ridicule that was heaped upon him in the saloons and dance halls, the countless times Jeff Thomas had risked his life fighting Russ' battles. He said, "If I was to go packin' a gun in a holster, I wouldn't live long enough to kill Dude Sudler. Thisaway, ever'body thinks I'm jist a ragged kid. Mostly now, they let me alone."

He reloaded the gun and fired again. He kept this up until he had shot away a full box of cartridges. Then, the oddly assorted pair mounted up and headed back to Cottonwood Springs.

Spring's warm sunshine melted the snow and dried the ground. Grass poked above it, lushly green. Flowers bloomed on the wide expanse of prairie. As the days passed, the tension began to build up in Russ. He followed the trail herds from Texas with his mind, counting each night's stop, imagining from Jeff's description of the countryside there when they crossed the Red, when they paused to pay toll to the Cherokees. He was expecting the first of the herds on the day the vanguard of them raised dust on the horizon.

But it was not the outfit of Dude Sudler, the man who had fomented the quarrel so long ago in front of the Mogollon Dance Palace. It was not the outfit of the man who had shouted as the nester's wagon drew abreast, "The marshal's gittin' away! Shoot, damn you, shoot!"

But activity in the town picked up. Marshal Jeff Thomas kept busy night-patrolling "Hide Park" and saloon row. And with him, like a shaggy, faithful dog, was always Russ Webber. Russ slouched. He shrank from attention. He kept his pale eyes on the ground. His hair was uncombed, his face unwashed. But somewhere in his tattered clothes nestled the bright, efficient Colt .45. And rankling in his heart was that wanton murder of a peaceful wagonload of settlers, his father, mother and brother.

A score of times each day he would mutter, "I'll kill him! I'll kill him! I'm good enough now. Why don't he come?"

He saw each new face in town and he kept searching. The townspeople thought him as harmless as the mayor's big shepherd dog. Pretty soon, they even stopped seeing him. He became a part of the marshal, as much a part as Jeff Thomas' twin sixguns, and not nearly so noticeable.

Dude Sudler's outfit hit Cottonwood Springs in the late evening. In the dark, nobody saw their coming. Dude and his crew came in about eight o'clock, leaving the herd with the night guards bedded half a dozen miles outside of town.

Jeff Thomas played poker in the Green Front saloon, and Russ Webber lounged beside the door, seeming half asleep, but not missing a face that passed through it. Jeff's luck was bad. Russ could see the flush of anger mounting into the handsome face, the darkly reckless look gathering behind his eyes.

Russ knew his friend had more to drink than was good for him. He could see it in the bloodshot eyes, in the slightly unsteady hands. He watched with a kind of fascination. A town marshal of Cottonwood Springs, Kansas, had no business drinking. It slowed his hands, unsteadied his aim.

And this concern for Jeff Thomas made him miss the crowd of dusty punchers that straggled noisily through the door, Dude Sudler among them. Dude, unnoticed, laid his washed-out, merciless eyes on Russ. His thin lips lifted their corners in a mirthless grin, and he looked away, no recognition lighting his evil face. He stood an arm's length away from the kid that had sworn to kill him, and surveyed the crowd.

The marshal's eyes were on the hand he had just drawn. A scowl deepened his features. As Dude saw him, a wild light came into his eyes. Nudging the men on either side of him, he growled, "There he is. He's been drinkin'. This ought to be easy."

Unobtrusively, he stalked through the crowd, four men behind him. In front of the marshal's table he stopped, his back to the door and to young Russ Webber. Russ still watched Jeff Thomas, only concern in his eyes.

Suddenly, Dude yelled, "You damn dirty skunk! I'm gonna blow the top of your head off!"

Russ jumped. He looked at the man, disbelief in his eyes, but still no recognition. Well, Jeff Thomas could handle this kind.

A gun leaped from the stranger's holster. Jeff Thomas started to get up. He grabbed at his holsters, but he was looking down the barrel of Dude Sudler's gun. Dude yelled again, his voice rising over the babble of loud talk, "I missed you last summer on account o' that damned nester wagon. But I won't miss this time!" Russ caught the hate in Dude's tone, wondering at its cause.

Dude fired. Blood ran redly on the marshal's throat, and the shock of the bullet knocked him back, his chair crashing. Dead silence fell over the room, broken only by the scrambling sounds of the percentage girls and customers as they dived for safety, out of the door, behind the long bar.

Dude fired again. The marshal's body jumped. The dazed look suddenly left the eyes of the boy at the door. Dude's words had given him away. Russ stepped quickly to the door, slammed it, turned the key and put it in his pocket. Then, he swung around.

It was a scene that was engraved forever on his brain. Jeff Thomas lay bloody, dead on the floor beside an overturned poker table. Dude Sudler stood over him, still pumping bullets into the motionless body. Dude's villainous crew stood grinning behind him.

Now, another scene flashed brightly before Russ' eyes. A nester's wagon with a woman and child dead inside. A farmer, toil roughened but honest, kind, lying in the dusty street. And Dude Sudler running around the corner of Halliday's feed store, a smoking gun in his hand.

Somehow, the bright Colt came out of the boy's ragged garments. It leveled on Dude and began to speak. The first bullet caught Dude in the chest and he reeled away, to crash into the huddled onlookers and slump lifeless to the floor. But Russ was not finished. He couldn't quit. Guns came up in the hands of Sudler's four cronies, and the boy's Colt cracked again and again. Bullets whispered through the thin walls behind him. Russ had shot four times. Four men were down. The fifth had a look of sheer terror in his eyes as he turned, running, finding his way blocked by the packed crowd.

Russ' gun followed him, coughed at him, and the man went down. Someone shouted, "Gawd, shoot out the light!" The bartender's shotgun sprayed buckshot at the ceiling. The chandelier came crashing down.

The room turned black. Panic came with the darkness. Men fought, and women screamed. "Quiet, damn it! Quiet! It's all over. Git out t' the street, but take yer time!"

A badly frightened gambler fired a derringer at the door, hoping the bullet would find the murderous kid. A Texan's gun answered, and another. Women clawed toward the windows. Men cursed.

Russ unlocked the door and slipped quietly out. The street was nearly deserted. He moved to the hitchrail and untied Jeff Thomas' horse. Mounting, he moved silently up the street and into the night. He murmured, his youthful face strangely peaceful, "Now, pa, I'll take up a place an' put down roots. It's time."

Cottonwood Springs, Kansas, never knew what became of Russ. It was assumed that he was wounded and crawled off somewhere to die. But if you were to drive your car north along the highway from Cottonwood Springs for about forty miles, you'd come to a place with a neat white house on it and a sod shack that they use for a spud cellar. It stands off to the left of the road.

If it was in the afternoon of a warm spring day, you'd probably find a peaceful old man sitting on the porch, a corncob pipe smoldering between his teeth, telling hair-raising stories to his grandchildren. Russ Webber don't look his ninety-five.

Carnage in Fact and Fiction

In a book called *The Gunfighters* (Time-Life Books, 1974), Paul Trachtman relates the following "spectacular shoot-out that left six men dead at Newton, Kansas, in 1871":

> In Newton's brothel district, aptly named Hide Park, a group of cowboys had gathered outside a dance hall near the Atchison, Topeka and Santa Fe railroad tracks. Inside, an ex-railroad man named McCluskie, who had shot a cowboy in a quarrel some days before, was talking with employees of the road. Led by a Texan named Hugh Anderson, the cowboys moved into the hall, firing as they entered. McCluskie was shot in the neck, but as he fell, he kept firing his own revolver and wounded Anderson. At that moment, a gaunt youth—he looked to be no more than 18—locked the dance-hall door and began blazing away at the cowboys, killing four of them. When the smoke cleared, McCluskie's avenger could not be found. No one knew anything about him, except that his name was Riley—and that he was dying of tuberculosis. (p. 38)

A little arithmetic tells us that Patten's story takes place about the same time. It was published in 1950, and Russ Webber is ninety-five years old. That means he was born in 1855, and if he is fourteen at the time of the shoot-out, the year is 1869. There could have been cattle drives passing through "Cottonwood Springs" that year on their way to Abilene, which flourished as a trail town between 1867 and 1876. The only problem is Russ's revolver. If it is a .45 Colt and uses metal cartridges, as Patten writes, it didn't exist until 1873.

In his own short story about the Hide Park massacre, Patten takes an interesting approach: he decides to use a marshal as a main character. In the first exchange of gunfire the marshal acts believably by trying to avoid trouble. It is believable that people could be accidentally killed, and it is natural that Marshal Thomas would befriend the young orphan and watch over him.

Now comes Patten's problem. Thomas's role as a law officer puts the character in an awkward position. When Russ Webber meets up with Dude Sudler, Thomas can't arrest Russ, because he hasn't done anything. But he can't warn Sudler, either, because it could mean that even more bystanders would get shot in his jurisdiction.

If Russ succeeds in gunning Sudler down, would the marshal arrest him? It wouldn't seem right to have Russ become a prisoner, or even a hunted outlaw, just because he wanted revenge on the man who killed his family. That would not be a satisfactory outcome for the story. Even less satisfactory would be an ending in which it is the marshal who kills Sudler. In such a scenario, Thomas would suddenly become the focus of the story, and young Russ would be left out.

From the point of view of a fiction writer, Marshal Thomas has to be eliminated. Patten therefore decides that Thomas will have a few drinks and become so interested in his card game that he will be off guard. But could a frontier law officer really get killed that way? Well, it happened to a former marshal of nearby Abilene, in a Deadwood saloon in 1876, assassinated as he sat at a game of cards. His name was James Butler "Wild Bill" Hickok.

Frank O'Rourke

1916–1989

In a career spanning four decades, Frank O'Rourke published more than sixty works of fiction. The versatility that became a hallmark of O'Rourke's writing was demonstrated in the first short stories that appeared during the 1940s and 1950s in the *Saturday Evening Post*, *Collier's*, *Ladies' Home Journal*, and *Esquire*. His first book, *"E" Company*, was introduced by Simon and Schuster in 1945 as the work of a "fresh and outstanding talent."

His interest in the West led to the large body of adventure westerns he wrote during the 1950s. Called "gifted and illuminating tale-telling" by the *Los Angeles Examiner* and praised by the *New York Times Book Review* ("This column has never failed to give Frank O'Rourke top billing for his Westerns"), O'Rourke's popular westerns established his reputation as a master of the genre, overshadowing to a large degree his movement away from the traditional western, beginning in 1956 with *The Diamond Hitch*. Written during the years when the author was living in Taos, New Mexico, the novel grew out of his friendship with Doughbelly Price, a bronc rider and cowhand in the old days. *The Diamond Hitch* dealt with the realities of western range life and was the first of O'Rourke's western novels to rank as authentic Americana.

In 1957 O'Rourke began taking a closer look at the myths of the West with *Legend in the Dust*. A demythologizing of the cowboy hero, the novel was a psychological study of Billy the Kid as a true killer. It was followed by two modern westerns: *The Man Who Found His Way* (1957), about a Prohibition-era Taos bootlegger; and *The Last Ride* (1958), a story of working cowboys engaged in a wild horse roundup and the sixty-five-year-old head of the group who becomes obsessed with capturing a single magnificent stallion.

O'Rourke's historical novel of New Mexico, *The Far Mountains* (1958), received the Southwestern Library Association's 1958–1959 award "in recognition of literary excellence and contribution to the culture and heritage of the Southwest."

In the 1960s and 1970s, O'Rourke published a spy-suspense series under the pseudonym Patrick O'Malley and contemporary novels set in California and the Southwest. He drew on his Nebraska background in such novels as *Window in the Dark* (1960) and *The Bright Morning* (1963), a story of youth growing into young adulthood in the 1930s. *The Swift Runner* (1968), a story of the dying old West, is perhaps his most popular novel. Among the motion pictures from his books is the classic adventure film "The Professionals," based on *A Mule for the Marquesa* (1964).

Frank O'Rourke's last works were stories for children, the first of which, *Burton and Stanley*, was published in 1993 by David R. Godine, Boston. The *Seattle Times* review commented, "rarely does a book this original, this charming come along." *Burton and Stanley* was the recipient of a Parents' Choice Foundation story book award.

The Last Shot

John Brandon stopped that night in a stand of pines on the last, long slope above the Shovel valley, eating two sandwiches and drinking cold, flat coffee from his canteen. Darkness had settled when he spread one blanket under the pines and lay back, with the soft, grass-sweetened wind stirring the tree-tops above him, shaking the first dead leaves over his bed. His horse cropped grass with tired dignity about the perimeter of its stake rope. John Brandon thought of his younger brother and replaced this sad memory with the face of another man—the man he hoped to find in the town up this valley; and then, forcing body and mind into rest, he slept deeply through the early fall night.

He rode late the next morning, picking up a dusty wagon trail that brought him into the town of Bend during the noon hour. He stabled and cared for his horse in the livery barn on the north end of Bend's single business block, and followed the stableman into the dingy, unswept office. The stableman—an old, weathered man with the bright, inquisitive eyes of the small-town gossip-spreader—carried a floating aroma of nitrogen and stale barn smells in his clothing. Brandon had to start somewhere and the stableman was nearest at hand. Brandon sat in the bigger of two wire-tied kitchen chairs and started to roll a cigarette.

"Quiet little town," Brandon said.

"She is and she ain't."

Brandon said, "Been here long?"

"Ten years this winter."

Brandon said, "Then you know everybody, I reckon?"

"All the living and most of the dead," the stableman said. "You looking for somebody?"

"Why, yes," Brandon said mildly. "A pretty big fellow with curly black hair and a mustache. Nice-looking and wears good clothes with fine boots. Does that place him for you?"

"Sure," the stableman said. "That's Charley Cannady. Been here about six months, buying and selling stock and some land. A real nice fellow, Charley." The stableman stared innocently at Brandon. "Got business with him?"

"Yes," Brandon said.

The stableman frowned. "Hope Charley ain't in no trouble?"

"No trouble," Brandon said. "Where does he hang out?"

"Up to the hotel."

"Thanks," Brandon said. "You care if I sit around awhile? My legs are tired."

"Make yourself to home," the stableman said. "I got to see a fella. Anybody comes in, tell 'em I'll be right back."

"Take your time" Brandon told him. "I'll hold the place down until you get back."

He saw the avid curiosity rising in the stableman's eyes, that small lurking fear of any stranger riding into town and inquiring about a citizen in good standing; and with this fear lay the hope that something might happen to relieve the monotony. Brandon watched him step outside and walk from view. Alone in the musty office with horses moving lazily against stall boards behind the thin office wall, Brandon thought of the ten months he had spent in trailing one man, the work and time and grief compressed into those months. And now his man was no more than one block distant. Now he could take his time.

He heard boots on the board sidewalk; and then a man middle-aged and plump filled the street door of the office with his short, wide bulk. His eyes found Brandon and stared without interest as he said, "Howdy."

"Stableman's out," Brandon said. "Be back soon."

"I'm Meagher," the man said. "Town marshal."

Brandon saw the star then, half concealed by an open, sagging vest, and knew where the stableman had gone—directly to the marshal's office with information. Brandon wondered incuriously how many times this same tableau had been repeated in the past years. He said quietly. "My name is Brandon, Marshal. What's the trouble?"

"No trouble, Mr. Brandon."

"He told you fast enough," Brandon said.

Meagher reddened faintly and stepped into the office. He said, "What's your business with Cannady?"

"My own" Brandon said. "But seeing you're the law I'll make it plain. I plan on shooting him."

Meagher did not show surprise. He said. "Why?"

"He shot my brother," Brandon said. "I've been trailing him quite a spell."

"How long?"

"Ten months," Brandon said. "Maybe you figure I'm foolish to tell you, Marshal. Here's my papers from down home. I'm deputized legally and got a warrant to bring him back. You can wire the sheriff there if you want proof."

Meagher examined the faded, sharply creased papers and returned them. He said. "You want him legal, I take it."

"You read the warrant," Brandon said.

"Dead or alive?"

Brandon said, "You read the warrant."

Meagher breathed gustily and took another step into the office. "You got a warrant, but you don't figure on taking him back, do you? You want to shoot him right here?"

"I described my man," Brandon said gently. "Your errand boy verified it, and now you agree. He's here. I'll be seeing him."

"All right," Meagher said. "He's been here six months and doing fine. Getting married next week, matter of fact."

"Home-town girl?"

"Yes. He built a new house. All furnished and ready to live in. This will hurt the girl. She's a good girl."

"Better now than later," Brandon said. "Will you tell him I'm in town?"

"Can't we do this legal?" Meagher asked heavily. "Take him back to stand trial. If that was the only thing he done wrong, it might not be too late for him to square the debt."

"I didn't need to ride in and tell you," Brandon said. "I could get him on my own. I just want to make it clear. My brother had no gun that night. Understand?"

"No gun? But—"

"I know," Brandon said tonelessly. "You know this Cannady. He's good with a gun. No use arguing, Marshal."

"You won't change your mind?"

"No," Brandon said. "And I'll warn him. At six tonight, clear your street and send him out. I'll be here. I'll meet him."

Meagher glanced at the gun on Brandon's right leg. "You any good with that?"

"You been studying it ten minutes," Brandon said bluntly. "You knew before you asked. No, I'm no good with it."

"Then why—"

"I want it that way," Brandon said. "I'm giving him a fair chance, more than he gave my brother. He can't back down and save face. You want to tell him or do I?"

Meagher was completely serious now. "That's your job. I reckon I ought to stop you, but it wouldn't do no good. You'd just keep on till you got him."

"A good guess," Brandon said.

Meagher nodded and moved through the door, pausing on the sidewalk to look once more at Brandon's gun and shake his head with heavy bewilderment. Brandon waited in the office until the marshal's steps had died away to the south. They were replaced minutes later by the stableman's light, tapping feet; then Brandon stood quickly and faced the stableman in the door.

"That was fast work," Brandon said, "but let me tell you something. Just stay around here this afternoon, and stay away from my horse. I'll be back directly."

Brandon passed the suddenly frightened man and walked south along Bend's short business block. The marshal's office and the jail were on the same side of the street and fifty feet or so south of the livery barn; and standing in a weather-worn rectangular shape on the opposite corner, three stories high and needing paint, was the hotel. Brandon crossed over and entered the lobby, hearing the clatter of dishes and talking voices from the adjoining dining room. Brandon took a faded, dried-out leather chair against the north wall and sat quietly until these sounds had nearly died away. The clerk watched him incuriously from behind a small desk.

Brandon said, "Mr. Cannady in there?"

"I think so," the clerk said. "You want to see him?"

"Please," Brandon said mildly.

"I'll tell him," the clerk said. "He's almost done with dinner."

The clerk went into the dining room and returned immediately, saying, "He'll be right out." Brandon rose from the chair and moved closer to the connecting door, hearing boots scrape and chairs pushed back as the unseen men rose from their table and spoke together for a brief moment. One man left the dining room by the street door and another paused to exchange a pleasantry with the waitress and then entered the lobby. Brandon recognized his man.

"Cannady," he said.

Cannady smiled and extended one hand. "You wish to see me, sir?"

"Yes," Brandon said. "Don't you know me?"

Cannady frowned. "Can't seem to place you."

"My name is Brandon," Brandon said. "Does that help?"

Cannady was not wearing his gun at this noon hour, but one hand made an automatic, involuntary gesture toward his right leg. He stood alert and stiffly, understanding and remembrance masked behind sharp black eyes.

"Brandon?" he said then. "I don't know any Brandons, sir. There must be some mistake."

"Talk is a waste of time," Brandon said. "I'll be at the livery barn this afternoon. At six I'll step into the street. I expect you to do likewise from this hotel. Stop thinking about making a break. I've trailed you ten months. Run for it and you'll get no even chance next time."

"Look here—" Cannady said.

"You hear me," Brandon said stolidly. "Make a break and I'll use a rifle on you in the hills."

Cannady remembered him well enough, even though their meeting in the past had been a quick passage on the main street of Brandon's home town. It was through the close resemblance of Brandon to his younger brother that Cannady saw and compared and remembered. Brandon watched him search rapidly into the past and recall certain facts about the Brandons. As the marshall before him had done, Cannady glanced at the gun on Brandon's leg and noted that it was unpolished by use and riding much too high on Brandon's leg for a swift, accurate draw. Cannady was remembering that the Brandons were peaceable men who no longer used guns in settling their quarrels; and, knowing this, he lost all fear.

Brandon said again: "You hear me?"

"Certainly," Cannady said. "I will accommodate you at six with pleasure. I suppose it would do no good to repeat that your foolish brother pushed me into that fight?"

"I know how it happened," Brandon said. "Save your words. I'll see you at six."

"I'll explain to our marshal," Cannady said. "I don't want interference."

"No need," Brandon said. "I saw him."

Brandon was inwardly pleased to see the sudden fear on Cannady's face at mention of the marshal. No matter what it was, the hunt was finished. Brandon turned and walked from the hotel and north on the quiet street to the office of the livery barn. The stableman came from the alleyway, shaking straw from his thin shoulders, and pottered uncomfortably behind the desk.

"Swallow the talk," Brandon said curtly. "You wouldn't be having any more business around town, would you?"

"I reckon not," the man said.

"Then do your work," Brandon said, "and keep your mouth shut."

A man needed to go back, Brandon thought, and consider everything carefully before he went forth to finish anything. He had trailed Cannady for ten months with the memory of his younger brother clear in his mind; but now, in the last minutes before the end of the trail, it was only fair and wise to remember everything and make sure he was right. Brandon sat in the dirty office through the long afternoon, watching the town move sluggishly, thinking of his own home and the past.

South of here was another country in a sense, settled and done with the first wild rush of the bad ones such as Cannady. Brandon had almost forgotten how to draw his gun in the past five years except to use it to hammer staples and twist wire and shoot an occasional crippled animal. His own town had settled comfortably into the middle portion of any town's history, growing steadily with the addition of schools and churches and good people. Brandon had grown through the wild years, but his younger brother had come along too late for a real taste of this feeling, and the result showed up in him as it did in all the younger men on the range. Boys will be boys, the old-timers chuckled, watching the younger men ride fast and whoop it up on Saturday nights, taking their excess meanness out in fist fights that left them slightly battered but thoroughly cleansed of that wildness. A few men like Cannady still happened through the towns, though, and it was inevitable for the younger men to appraise them with a feeling of wonder and envy. Brandon's younger brother had been foolish to a certain degree, but he had never considered serious harm to any man.

Brandon had been hazing strays from the river bottom that week and had not ridden into town on Saturday night. His younger brother and the two hands left in later afternoon, after begging him half-heartedly to come along. They rode away in high spirits, dressed in their best, racing to a big night. Brandon watched them go and chuckled with the knowledge and stability of his thirty-five years. He knew the pattern of their night before they made the first move: riding fast down the main street, yelling sheer good humor, a couple of drinks at the Longhorn, and then the dance. And about five the next morning they would ride into Brandon's river camp with a great deal of unnecessary hullabaloo, waking him and retelling all the fights and flirtations and other gossip of the neighborhood. Brandon's younger brother was interested in a town girl and would moon around for a day, thinking about her. Brandon knew the girl was an empty-headed little fool, but it was useless to give warning. His brother would discover it for himself in due time.

Five old friends rode into the river camp just after three o'clock, and they woke him without shouts or laughter. He sat up in his blankets and stared above the hastily kindled fire and missed his brother's face. They told him what had happened while he slipped into his boots and saddled his horse for the ride to town. His brother had been shot by a stranger named Charles Chambers. Brandon had seen Chambers in town a week ago, in the Longhorn, but had not spoken to the man. It seemed that Chambers had kept company with young Brandon's girl for several evenings prior to the Saturday night dance. Brandon's younger brother exchanged hot words with Chambers on the dance floor, and Chambers said, "Shut up, kid. Grow up and then come around." That was more than enough for a hot-headed fool, even though Chambers wore a gun and knew how to use it. Chambers escorted the girl to her home at midnight and Brandon's younger brother followed. His friends tagged along to watch the expected fist fight. Chambers was in the kitchen with the girl, his horse tied out back, his equipment ready for a long ride. Brandon's younger brother knocked on the kitchen door and shouted at Chambers to come out and fight like a man. Chambers told him to go away, and Brandon's younger brother answered that he was coming in. He was not wearing a gun. When he slammed the door open and stood in the doorway, Chambers lifted a shotgun from beside the kitchen chair and shot him. By the time the other young men reached the house, the girl was screaming and Chambers had gone.

Brandon rode thirty miles to town without speaking. He stayed with his brother until the inevitable happened and then did the only thing a man could do. He knew his younger brother had been foolish and rash, but he had not carried a gun and Chambers knew this. The county sheriff deputized Brandon and wrote out the warrant. Brandon went home and made arrangements for the future. His older brother and two uncles would take care of the ranch work, and the neighbors would help. Brandon started on the trail that night. He had ridden ever since, following the cold trace, the little clues, the gradually warming scent of his man. He had given himself a year; now two months were on the credit side of the ledger.

He had lost weight during this time. He had been a tall and somewhat bulky man, but he had sloughed off his excess weight until he was pared down to muscle and bone—a sober-faced man with a three-day growth of black whiskers partially hiding his square jaw and weather-darkened face. He wore the same heavy leather chaps he had started with, buckled above the knee and frayed from endless days of riding over all kinds of country. Those chaps in this higher grassland were out of place, but sitting quietly in the sun-heated, smelly office, Brandon made no move to remove them and give his legs the additional freedom needed at six o'clock.

People had gone about their daily business during the afternoon, talking on the street, going and coming, moving unhurriedly through the town. A few wagons rattled in from the west and south, and saddle horses lined the rail before the saloon adjoining the hotel. People were pretty much the same anywhere a man rode, he thought, living out their days in the same jobs and pleasures. This town of Bend was no different from his own town so far away; it would grow more in the next few years and add churches and schools and bigger houses. The marshall would put his gun away and walk the streets without fear of men like Cannady who changed their names to suit their purpose. That would be the best time for the town and its people, he thought, and for all towns and all people.

The marshal did not appear during the afternoon. Cannady came from the hotel at four o'clock and drove past the livery barn in a light buggy, turning north on the last side street toward an unseen house. He returned in an hour and entered the hotel. The stableman pottered around the barn, doing nothing and listening closely. After five o'clock, people began drifting downtown and gathering in the saloons and stores. They had got the news on the invisible grapevine and were waiting for the show. He would not disappoint them, Brandon thought grimly, but might surprise them.

Time was short now. He had reviewed everything and could not see a better way to end the hunt. He had been right from the beginning; his heart, beating steadily without excitement, told him that. He rolled a last cigarette and smoked it deliberately, watching the sun fall lower in the far west.

At exactly ten minutes of six, Brandon walked into the barn alley and said, "Go into your office and stay there." He waited until the stableman scuttled past him and ducked through the inner door. Then he went to his stall and patted his horse gently, murmuring, "Easy, boy, easy."

The horse nuzzled his shoulder while Brandon saddled and checked all gear twice. He led the horse into the alley, facing the rear door, and tied the reins in a loose slip-knot to the last brace post beside the door. He was standing in deep shadow when he pulled the stubby, double-barreled shotgun from its saddle holster. He inspected two shells and went on to a detailed

and careful examination of the shotgun, snapping both triggers and check-
ing the firing pins before loading both barrels and closing the breech. He
cocked both triggers, grasped the shotgun by its carved pistol grip, and
placed the stock under his arm, against his body, the butt pushed into his
armpit, the forearm and barrels pressed firmly against his left leg. The
sweat-stiffened wings of his leather chaps and his loose shirt sleeve hid the
shotgun from front view. He had practiced this many times and knew exactly how to hold the shotgun. He did not check his revolver in the awkward
holster tied against his right leg.

Brandon walked slowly to the barn door facing the street and paused,
looking north and south. He saw the stableman's expectant face framed in
the office's one dirty window, jerking back quickly as Brandon looked his
way. Brandon walked into the street, to the exact center, and faced south;
and at this moment Cannady stepped briskly from the hotel veranda and
faced north in the center of the street. Brandon estimated the intervening
distance at about one hundred steps. The street was empty, but people stood
behind every window and door, and one kill-hungry man was straddling the
saloon roof.

Brandon walked twenty steps down the street and stopped just before he
came abreast of the marshal's office. Meagher stood in his doorway, hand on
hips, staring moodily at Brandon. He called in a gentle voice: "You won't re-
consider, Brandon?"

"Sorry," Brandon said. "Stay where you are."

Brandon waited in this spot and saw Cannady laugh and move forward
quickly, right arm hanging in a fixed arc at his side. In this moment, Brandon saw a girl come from the hotel and stand on the veranda. She was a slen-
der and delicately featured woman with dark hair, and she lifted one hand to
her mouth and leaned stiffly against the weathered, knife-whittled railing in
a position of fear. Brandon saw her, knew who she was immediately, and
thought of the girl in his home town and of other girls who must be living in
other towns, remembering Cannady and nursing the thinly healed scars of
old, bitter memory. He could see them as they lived, forgotten by Cannady;
but watching this woman, he understood why Cannady had stayed on in
Bend. She was the woman Cannady had searched for; and, having discovered something as good and decent as she was, he had pushed his old life behind and had begun a new one. But too late.

Brandon stood without arm movement, watching the distance between
them decrease to sixty, fifty, nearly thirty paces. Then Cannady stopped, his
face clear and bright in the first soft evening shadow. "Make your play,
Brandon," he called sharply.

"Come on," Brandon said. "Come on."

"An old trick," Cannady said, "I've come my half. Your turn now, Brandon. But I'll tell you something. Take five steps and stop. Then go for your gun."

"All right," Brandon said. "I'll call that bluff. I knew you were a coward before. Now I'm sure. I'm wondering which step you'll draw on to catch me off balance. You wouldn't be thinking of that, would you?"

Brandon did not wait for words. He walked forward stiffly and, reaching his third step, tensed his left arm as his leg lifted and moved forward into the fourth step. He stopped suddenly and dropped into a crouch and swung the shotgun up from behind the leather chap, level with his hips, right arm coming across and steadying the barrels. He pulled both triggers at the apex of this swift movement, just before Cannady made his draw. Through the heavy, simultaneous reports, the smoke, and the recoil, Brandon saw the buckshot sweep Cannady from his feet and smash him face down in the street's brown dust. The half-drawn gun spun from lax fingers as Cannady screamed. Behind Brandon, the marshal called hoarsely and came in a heavy, angry rush, shouting: "I knew you had something figured, you—!"

Brandon reloaded the shotgun as he turned to face the marshal. He said coldly, "He won't die. I shot him in the legs."

People were running into the street. The town doctor came through this thickening crowd with his black bag and dropped on both knees beside Cannady. The marshal spoke with a raging fury: "A damned shotgun. Look at his legs. He'll never walk again. You know what buckshot does close up. He'll lose both of 'em. Brandon, you're under arrest. Drop that gun."

Brandon lifted the shotgun and stopped Meagher's hand midway in its flight to the holster. Brandon said, "Listen to me, Meagher. He shot my brother in the legs with a shotgun. My brother had no gun. My brother's alive, sure, with one leg. You can check on that, Meagher. I told you I would shoot him. I didn't say kill him. I didn't say what with. This is how I've wanted it for ten months; this is the way it had to be. He's no good, Meagher. He's a coward and a killer, and I want him like this for the rest of his life, and I hope he lives a hundred years."

"I—" Meagher said, and turned away, head low on his chest. "I believe you, Brandon. Everything else checked like you told me."

"I'm riding," Brandon said. "You figure on stopping me?"

"No," Meagher said. "Not now."

Brandon lowered the shotgun and stepped beside the doctor and the man, groaning now in the street's thick dust. Brandon said, "Will he live?"

The doctor did not look up. He said, "Of course he'll live, without the right leg, maybe part of the left. Get a stretcher, you fools. I've got to move this man."

Brandon stepped back and watched them carry Cannady into the hotel. Only then did he turn and say, "Walk along to the barn with me, Meagher."

They pushed through an angry crowd of uncertain, babbling people, into the darkness of the barn alley. Brandon pushed the shotgun into its saddle holster and untied his horse. He said then, "Thanks for understanding, Meagher."

"I got to," Meagher said. "I got to thank you, too. I knew what he was when he came up the street. I've seen a lot of them in my time, Brandon. When they get ready to draw, they show a lot in their eyes."

"Gracias," Brandon said softly.

He mounted and leaned forward in the saddle, a last thought stirring and bothering his mind. He said, "That girl he was marrying tomorrow. I hope you give her the straight of it."

"I will," Meagher said. "That's why I'm thanking you."

"You know her?" Brandon asked.

"My daughter," Meagher said. "You better ride, Brandon. He had a few friends in town. I got to get home."

Brandon began words and shut them off deep in his throat. He rode from the back door of the livery barn, east from the town into open range, then south toward the distant rising ridges. Two hours later, stopping beside a small creek to blow his horse and listen, he drew the shotgun from his saddle holster and dropped it into the creek before riding on.

Fair Revenge, Western Style

"Beware of punishing wrongfully; do not kill, for it will not profit you." — Egyptian manuscript, ca. 2135 B.C.

"Eye for eye, tooth for tooth, hand for hand, foot for foot." — *Exodus* 21:24

"And if you wrong us, shall we not revenge?" — Shakespeare, *The Merchant of Venice*, act 5, scene 1

Looking at these quotations, we can assume that revenge is one of the oldest themes in literature. Shakespeare used it in *Hamlet*, which ends up with more corpses than a saloon shootout. In *Paradise Lost* Milton dramatizes the human problems that began when Satan wanted revenge against God and chose the Garden of Eden as his target.

In the history of the American West, vengeance certainly plays a big part. Hundreds of stories were inspired by the individuals—and the groups—who set out to "get even" and ended up fighting the Lincoln County War in 1878 and the Johnson County War in 1892. There was a drawn-out vendetta down in Texas in the 1870s known as the Sutton-Taylor Feud, which involved John Wesley Hardin. Arizona had the Graham-Tewksbury feud in the 1890s.

Revenge offers a writer some interesting options when it comes time for the story to reach its climax. For example, the hero might get vengeance but be killed in the process. Or the avenger can have a change of heart, discovering that forgiveness is a better kind of victory. Or it can turn out that the whole thing was a big misunderstanding. The writer might even arrange things so that the bad person is punished but the good person does not have to commit murder and end up a criminal.

Frank O'Rourke provides a new twist on the plot by having deputy John Brandon pull out a concealed sawed-off shotgun instead of a Colt revolver. And in another interesting twist, it turns out that the villain's next victim would have been the marshal's daughter. When we learn *that*, we have to go back and look again at what Marshal Meagher says and does. Did he have a motive in letting Brandon go ahead?

The title is interesting, too. There are no clues to tell us when the story takes place—no references to specific types of guns, for instance, or references to anything we could put a date on. But it seems to be a time when the frontier life was nearly over: "South of here was another country in a sense, settled and done with the first wild rush of the bad ones such as Cannady . . . . His own town had settled comfortably into the middle portion of any town's history."

Revenge will probably always remain a part of human life. But the West did change, as shown in this story. The rough little towns that started out "wild" and free, as places where people took care of revenge personally, became civilized. They settled down and left such matters in the hands of lawfully appointed peace officers. O'Rourke chose the title of this story because Brandon finishes a fight that started with his brother and Cannady. But the title also seems to say that an era is over, and that this is the last shot in one of the last feuds of the old wild West.

Donald Hamilton

b. 1916

"The Guns of William Longley" appeared in a 1967 Western Writers of America anthology titled *Iron Men and Silver Spurs* and won the WWA Spur Award for the best short story of the year. This came as a surprise to some readers who thought that Hamilton wrote only spy novels about a character named Matt Helm.

Two of Hamilton's western novels have been made into films: *Smoky Valley* (1954), which became the film *The Violent Men*, and *The Big Country* (1957). His other westerns are *Mad River* (1956), *The Man from Santa Clara* (1960, reprinted as *The Two-Shoot Gun* in 1971), and *Texas Fever* (1961).

In Hamilton's western stories we find many heroes like the one in "The Guns of William Longley." They know their own strengths and weaknesses, and they don't need to rely on outside help or special weapons. They also know enough to stay out of trouble until it is forced upon them.

Hamilton's biggest success came in 1960, when he published *Death of a Citizen* and thereby introduced his readers to Matt Helm, who would go on to become the hero in more than two dozen novels. Many readers who have never heard of Hamilton's westerns can recognize such titles as *The Wrecking Crew* (1960), *Murderer's Row* (1962), *The Annihilators* (1983), and *The Demolishers* (1987). *Contemporary Authors* calls Matt Helm "one of the most popular secret agent characters ever created," and a *New York Times* reviewer credits Hamilton for his "authentic, hard realism." That holds true for "The Guns of William Longley," too.

The Guns of William Longley

We'd been up north delivering a herd for old man Butcher the summer I'm telling about. I was nineteen at the time. I was young and big, and I was plenty tough, or thought I was, which amounts to the same thing up to a point. Maybe I was making up for all the years of being that nice Anderson boy, back in Willow Fork, Texas. When your dad wears a badge, you're kind of obliged to behave yourself around home so as not to shame him. But Pop was dead now, and this wasn't Texas.

Anyway, I was tough enough that we had to leave Dodge City in something of a hurry after I got into an argument with a fellow who, it turned out, wasn't nearly as handy with a gun as he claimed to be. I'd never killed a man before. It made me feel kind of funny for a couple of days, but like I say, I was young and tough then, and I'd seen men I really cared for trampled in stampedes and drowned in rivers on the way north. I wasn't going to grieve long over one belligerent stranger.

It was on the long trail home that I first saw the guns one evening by the fire. We had a blanket spread on the ground, and we were playing cards for what was left of our pay—what we hadn't already spent on girls and liquor and general hell-raising. My luck was in, and one by one the others dropped out, all but Waco Smith, who got stubborn and went over to his bedroll and hauled out the guns.

"I got them in Dodge," he said. "Pretty, ain't they? Fellow I bought them from claimed they belonged to Bill Longley."

"Is that a fact?" I said, like I wasn't much impressed. "Who's Longley?"

I knew who Bill Longley was, all right, but a man's got a right to dicker a bit, and besides I couldn't help deviling Waco now and then. I liked him all right, but he was one of those cocky little fellows who ask for it. You know the kind. They always know everything.

I sat there while he told me about Bill Longley, the giant from Texas with thirty-two killings to his credit, the man who was hanged twice. A bunch of vigilantes strung him up once for horse-stealing he hadn't done, but the rope broke after they'd ridden off and he dropped to the ground, kind of short of breath but alive and kicking.

Then he was tried and hanged for a murder he had done, some years later in Giddings, Texas. He was so big that the rope gave way again and he landed on his feet under the trap, making six-inch-deep footprints in the hard ground—they're still there in Giddings to be seen, Waco said, Bill Longley's footprints—but it broke his neck this time and they buried him nearby. At least a funeral service was held, but some say there's just an empty coffin in the grave.

I said, "This Longley gent can't have been so much, to let folks keep stringing him up that way."

That set Waco off again, while I toyed with the guns. They were pretty, all right, in a big carved belt with two carved holsters, but I wasn't much interested in leather-work. It was the weapons themselves that took my fancy. They'd been used but someone had looked after them well. They were handsome pieces, smooth-working, and they had a good feel to them. You know how it is when a firearm feels just right. A fellow with hands the size of mine doesn't often find guns to fit him like that.

"How much do you figure they're worth?" I asked, when Waco stopped for breath.

"Well, now," he said, getting a sharp look on his face, and I came home to Willow Fork with the Longley guns strapped around me. If that's what they were.

I got a room and cleaned up at the hotel. I didn't much feel like riding clear out to the ranch and seeing what it looked like with Ma and Pa gone two years and nobody looking after things. Well, I'd put the place on its feet again one of these days, as soon as I'd had a little fun and saved a little money. I'd buckle right down to it, I told myself, as soon as Junellen set the date, which I'd been after her to do since before my folks died. She couldn't keep saying forever we were too young.

I got into my good clothes and went to see her. I won't say she'd been on my mind all the way up the trail and back again, because it wouldn't be true. A lot of the time I'd been too busy or tired for dreaming, and in Dodge City I'd done my best *not* to think of her, if you know what I mean. It did seem like a young fellow engaged to a beautiful girl like Junellen Barr could have behaved himself better up there, but it had been a long dusty drive and you know how it is.

But now I was home and it seemed like I'd been missing Junellen every minute since I left, and I couldn't wait to see her. I walked along the street in the hot sunshine feeling light and happy. Maybe my leaving my guns at the hotel had something to do with the light feeling, but the happiness was all for Junellen, and I ran up the steps to the house and knocked on the door. She'd have heard we were back and she'd be waiting to greet me, I was sure.

I knocked again and the door opened and I stepped forward eagerly. "Junellen—" I said, and stopped foolishly.

"Come in, Jim," said her father, a little turkey of a man who owned the drygoods store in town. He went on smoothly: "I understand you had quite an eventful journey. We are waiting to hear all about it."

He was being sarcastic, but that was his way, and I couldn't be bothered with trying to figure what he was driving at. I'd already stepped into the room, and there was Junellen with her mother standing close as if to protect her, which seemed kind of funny. There was a man in the room, too, Mister Carmichael from the bank, who'd fought with Pa in the war. He was tall and handsome as always, a little heavy nowadays but still dressed like a fashion plate. I couldn't figure what he was doing there.

It wasn't going at all the way I'd hoped, my reunion with Junellen, and I stopped, looking at her.

"So you're back, Jim," she said. "I heard you had a real exciting time. Dodge City must be quite a place."

There was a funny hard note in her voice. She held herself very straight, standing there by her mother, in a blue-flowered dress that matched her eyes. She was a real little lady, Junellen. She made kind of a point of it, in fact, and Martha Butcher, old man Butcher's kid, used to say about Junellen Barr that butter wouldn't melt in her mouth, but that always seemed like a silly saying to me, and who was Martha Butcher anyway, just because her daddy owned a lot of cows?

Martha'd also remarked about girls who had to drive two front names in harness as if one wasn't good enough, and I'd told her it surely wasn't if it was a name like Martha, and she'd kicked me on the shin. But that was a long time ago when we were all kids.

Junellen's mother broke the silence, in her nervous way: "Dear, hadn't you better tell Jim the news?" She turned to Mister Carmichael. "Howard, perhaps you should—"

Mister Carmichael came forward and took Junellen's hand. "Miss Barr has done me the honor to promise to be my wife," he said.

I said, "But she can't. She's engaged to me."

Junellen's mother's mother said quickly, "It was just a childish thing, not to be taken seriously."

I said, "Well, I took it seriously!"

Junellen looked up at me. "Did you, Jim? In Dodge City, did you?" I didn't say anything. She said breathlessly, "It doesn't matter. I suppose I could forgive. . . . But you have killed a man. I could never love a man who has taken a human life."

Anyway, she said something like that. I had a funny feeling in my stomach and a roaring sound in my ears. They talk about your heart breaking, but that's where it hit me, the stomach and the ears. So I can't tell you exactly what she said, but it was something like that.

I heard myself say, "Mister Carmichael spent the war peppering Yanks with a pea-shooter, I take it."

"That's different—"

Mister Carmichael spoke quickly. "What Miss Barr means is that there's a difference between a battle and a drunken brawl, Jim. I am glad your father did not live to see his son wearing two big guns and shooting men down in the street. He was a fine man and a good sheriff for this county. It was only for his memory's sake that I agreed to let Miss Barr break the news to you in person. From what we hear of your exploits up north, you have certainly forfeited all right to consideration from her."

There was something in what he said, but I couldn't see that it was his place to say it. "You agreed?" I said. "That was mighty kind of you sir, I'm sure." I looked away from him. "Junellen—"

Mister Carmichael interrupted. "I do not wish my fiancée to be distressed by a continuation of this painful scene. I must ask you to leave, Jim."

I ignored him. "Junellen," I said, "is this what you really—"

Mister Carmichael took me by the arm. I turned my head to look at him again. I looked at the hand with which he was holding me. I waited. He didn't let go. I hit him and he went back across the room and kind of fell into a chair. The chair broke under him. Junellen's father ran over to help him up. Mr. Carmichael's mouth was bloody. He wiped it with a handkerchief.

I said, "You shouldn't have put your hand on me, sir."

"Note the pride," Mr. Carmichael said, dabbing at his cut lip. "Note the vicious, twisted pride. They all have it, all these young toughs. You are too big for me to box, Jim, and it is an undignified thing, anyway. I have worn a sidearm in my time. I will go to the bank and get it, while you arm yourself."

"I will meet you in front of the hotel, sir," I said, "if that is agreeable to you."

"It is agreeable," he said, and went out.

I followed him without looking back. I think Junellen was crying, and I know her parents were saying one thing and another in high, indignant voices, but the funny roaring was in my ears and I didn't pay too much attention. The sun was very bright outside. As I started for the hotel, somebody ran up to me.

"Here you are, Jim." It was Waco, holding out the Longley guns in their carved holsters. "I heard what happened. Don't take any chances with the old fool."

I looked down at him and asked, "How did Junellen and her folks learn about what happened in Dodge?"

He said, "It's a small town, Jim, and all the boys have been drinking and talking, glad to get home."

"Sure," I said, buckling on the guns. "Sure."

It didn't matter. It would have got around sooner or later, and I wouldn't have lied about it if asked. We walked slowly toward the hotel.

"Dutch LeBaron is hiding out back in the hills with a dozen men," Waco said. "I heard it from a man in a bar."

"Who's Dutch LeBaron?" I asked. I didn't care, but it was something to talk about as we walked.

"Dutch?" Waco said. "Why Dutch is wanted in five states and a couple of territories. Hell, the price on his head is so high now even Fenn is after him."

"Fenn?" I said. He sure knew a lot of names. "Who's Fenn?"

"You've heard of Old Joe Fenn, the bounty hunter. Well, if he comes after Dutch, he's asking for it. Dutch can take care of himself."

"Is that a fact?" I said, and then I saw Mr. Carmichael coming, but he was a ways off yet and I said, "You sound like this Dutch fellow was a friend of yours—"

But Waco wasn't there any more. I had the street to myself, except for Mr. Carmichael, who had a gun strapped on outside his fine coat. It was an army gun in a black army holster with a flap, worn cavalry style on the right side, butt forward. They wear them like that to make room for the saber on the left, but it makes a clumsy rig.

I walked forward to meet Mr. Carmichael, and I knew I would have to let him shoot once. He was a popular man and a rich man and he would have to draw first and shoot first or I would be in serious trouble. I figured it all out very coldly, as if I had been killing men all my life. We stopped, and Mr. Carmichael undid the flap of the army holster and pulled out the big cavalry pistol awkwardly and fired and missed, as I had known, somehow, that he would.

Then I drew the right-hand gun, and as I did so I realized that I didn't particularly want to kill Mr. Carmichael. I mean, he was a brave man coming here with his old cap-and-ball pistol, knowing all the time that I could outdraw and outshoot him with my eyes closed. But I didn't want to be killed, either, and he had the piece cocked and was about to fire again. I tried to aim for a place that wouldn't kill him, or cripple him too badly, and the gun wouldn't do it.

I mean, it was a frightening thing. It was like I was fighting the Longley gun for Mr. Carmichael's life. The old army revolver fired once more and something rapped my left arm lightly. The Longley gun went off at last, and Mr. Carmichael spun around and fell on his face in the street. There was a cry, and Junellen came running and went to her knees beside him.

"You murderer!" she screamed at me. "You hateful murderer!"

It showed how she felt about him, that she would kneel in the dust like that in her blue-flowered dress. Junellen was always very careful of her pretty clothes. I punched out the empty and replaced it. Dr. Sims came up and examined Mr. Carmichael and said he was shot in the leg, which I already knew, being the one who had shot him there. Dr. Sims said he was going to be all right, God willing.

Having heard this, I went over to another part of town and tried to get drunk. I didn't have much luck at it, so I went into the place next to the hotel for a cup of coffee. There wasn't anybody in the place but a skinny girl with an apron on.

I said, "I'd like a cup of coffee, ma'am," and sat down.

She said, coming over, "Jim Anderson, you're drunk. At least you smell like it."

I looked up and saw that it was Martha Butcher. She set a cup down in front of me. I asked, "What are you doing here waiting tables?"

She said, "I had a fight with Dad about . . . well, never mind what it was about. Anyway, I told him I was old enough to run my own life and if he didn't stop trying to boss me around like I was one of the hands, I'd pack up and leave. And he laughed and asked what I'd do for money, away from home, and I said I'd earn it, so here I am."

It was just like Martha Butcher, and I saw no reason to make a fuss over it like she probably wanted me to.

"Seems like you are," I agreed. "Do I get sugar, too, or does that cost extra?"

She laughed and set a bowl in front of me. "Did you have a good time in Dodge?" she asked.

"Fine," I said. "Good liquor. Fast games. Pretty girls. Real pretty girls."

"Fiddlesticks," she said. "I know what you think is pretty. Blonde and simpering. You big fool. If you'd killed him over her they'd have put you in jail, at the very least. And just what are you planning to use for an arm when that one gets rotten and falls off? Sit still."

She got some water and cloth and fixed up my arm where Mr. Carmichael's bullet had nicked it.

"Have you been out to your place yet?" she asked.

I shook my head. "Figure there can't be much out there by now. I'll get after it one of these days."

"One of these days!" she said. "You mean when you get tired of strutting around with those big guns and acting dangerous—" She stopped abruptly.

I looked around, and got to my feet. Waco was there in the doorway, and with him was a big man, not as tall as I was, but wider. He was a real whiskery gent, with a mat of black beard you could have used for stuffing a mattress. He wore two gunbelts, crossed, kind of sagging low at the hips.

Waco said, "You're a fool to sit with your back to the door, Jim. That's the mistake Hickok made, remember? If instead of us it had been somebody like Jack McCall—"

"Who's Jack McCall?" I asked innocently.

"Why, he's the fellow shot Wild Bill in the back . . ." Waco's face reddened. "All right, all right. Always kidding me. Dutch, this big joker is my partner, Jim Anderson, Jim, Dutch LeBaron. He's got a proposition for us."

I tried to think back to where Waco and I had decided to become partners, and couldn't remember the occasion. Well, maybe it happens like that, but it seemed like I should have had some say in it.

"Your partner tells me you're pretty handy with those guns," LeBaron said, after Martha'd moved off across the room. "I can use a man like that."

"For what?" I asked.

"For making some quick money over in New Mexico Territory," he said.

I didn't ask any fool questions, like whether the money was to be made legally or illegally. "I'll think about it," I said.

Waco caught my arm. "What's to think about? We'll be rich, Jim!"

I said, "I'll think about it, Waco."

LeBaron said, "What's the matter, sonny, are you scared?"

I turned to look at him. He was grinning at me, but his eyes weren't grinning, and his hands weren't too far from those low-slung guns.

I said, "Try me and see."

I waited a little. Nothing happened. I walked out of there and got my pony and rode out to the ranch, reaching the place about dawn. I opened the door and stood there, surprised. It looked just about the way it had when the folks were alive, and I half expected to hear Ma yelling at me to beat the dust off outside and not bring it into the house. Somebody had cleaned the place up for me, and I thought I knew who. Well, it certainly was neighborly of her, I told myself. It was nice to have somebody show a sign they were glad to have me home, even if it was only Martha Butcher.

I spent a couple of days out there, resting up and riding around. I didn't find much stock. It was going to take money to make a going ranch of it again, and I didn't figure my credit at Mr. Carmichael's bank was anything to count on. I couldn't help giving some thought to Waco and LeBaron and the proposition they'd put before me. It was funny, I'd think about it most when I had the guns on. I was out back practicing with them one day when the stranger rode up.

He was a little, dry, elderly man on a sad-looking white horse he must have hired at the livery stable for not very much, and he wore his gun in front of his left hip with the butt to the right for a cross draw. He didn't make any noise coming up. I'd fired a couple of times before I realized he was there.

"Not bad," he said when he saw me looking at him. "Do you know a man named LeBaron, son?"

"I've met him," I said.

"Is he here?"

"Why should he be here?"

"A bartender in town told me he'd heard you and your sidekick, Smith, had joined up with LeBaron, so I thought you might have given him the use of your place. It would be more comfortable for him than hiding out in the hills."

"He isn't here," I said. The stranger glanced toward the house. I started to get mad, but shrugged instead. "Look around if you want to."

"In that case," he said, "I don't figure I want to." He glanced toward the target I'd been shooting at, and back to me. "Killed a man in Dodge, didn't you son? And then stood real calm and let a fellow here in town fire three shots at you, after which you laughed and pinked him neatly in the leg."

"I don't recall laughing," I said. "And it was two shots, not three."

"It makes a good story, however," he said. "And it is spreading. You have a reputation already, did you know that, Anderson? I didn't come here just to look for LeBaron. I figured I'd like to have a look at you, too. I always like to look up fellows I might have business with later."

"Business?" I said, and then I saw that he'd taken a tarnished old badge out of his pocket and was pinning it on his shirt. "Have you a warrant, sir?" I asked.

"Not for you," he said. "Not yet."

He swung the old white horse around and rode off. When he was out of sight, I got my pony out of the corral. It was time I had a talk with Waco. Maybe I was going to join LeBaron and maybe I wasn't, but I didn't much like his spreading it around before it was true.

I didn't have to look for him in town. He came riding to meet me with three companions, all hard ones if I ever saw any.

"Did you see Fenn?" he shouted as he came up. "Did he come this way?"

"A little old fellow with some kind of a badge?" I said. "Was that Fenn? He headed back to town, about ten minutes ahead of me. He didn't look like much."

"Neither does the devil when he's on business," Waco said. "Come on, we'd better warn Dutch before he rides into town."

I rode along with them, and we tried to catch LeBaron on the trail, but he'd already passed with a couple of men. We saw their dust ahead and chased it, but they made it before us, and Fenn was waiting in front of the cantina that was LeBaron's hangout when he was in town.

We saw it all as we came pounding after LeBaron, who dismounted and started into the place, but Fenn came forward, looking small and inoffensive. He was saying something and holding out his hand. LeBaron stopped and shook hands with him, and the little man held onto LeBaron's hand, took a step to the side, and pulled his gun out of the cross-draw holster left-handed, with a kind of twisting motion.

Before LeBaron could do anything with his free hand, the little old man had brought the pistol barrel down across his head. It was as neat and cold-blooded a thing as you'd care to see. In an instant, LeBaron was unconscious on the ground, and Old Joe Fenn was covering the two men who'd been riding with him.

Waco Smith, riding beside me, made a sort of moaning sound as if he'd been clubbed himself. "Get him!" he shouted, drawing his gun. "Get the dirty sneaking bounty hunter!"

I saw the little man throw a look over his shoulder, but there wasn't much

he could do about us with those other two to handle. I guess he hadn't figured us for reinforcements riding in. Waco fired and missed. He never could
shoot much, particularly from horseback. I reached out with one of the guns
and hit him over the head before he could shoot again. He spilled from the
saddle.

I didn't have it all figured out. Certainly it wasn't a very nice thing Mr.
Fenn had done, first taking a man's hand in friendship and then knocking
him unconscious. Still, I didn't figure LeBaron had ever been one for giving
anybody a break; and there was something about the old fellow standing
there with his tarnished old badge that reminded me of Pa, who'd died
wearing a similar piece of tin on his chest. Anyway, there comes a time in a
man's life when he's got to make a choice, and that's the way I made mine.

Waco and I had been riding ahead of the others. I turned my pony fast
and covered them with the guns as they came charging up—as well as you
can cover anybody from a plunging horse. One of them had his pistol aimed
to shoot. The left-hand Longley gun went off, and he fell to the ground. I
was kind of surprised. I'd never been much at shooting left-handed. The
other two riders veered off and headed out of town.

By the time I got my pony quieted down from having that gun go off in
his ear, everything was pretty much under control. Waco had disappeared,
so I figured he couldn't be hurt much; and the new sheriff was there, old
drunken Billy Bates who'd been elected after Pa's death by the gambling element in town, who hadn't liked the strict way Pa ran things.

"I suppose it's legal," Old Billy was saying grudgingly. "But I don't take
it kindly, Marshal, your coming here to serve a warrant without letting me
know."

"My apologies, Sheriff," Fenn said smoothly. "An oversight, I assure
you. Now, I'd like a wagon. He's worth seven-hundred and fifty dollars over
in New Mexico Territory."

"No decent person would want that kind of money," Old Billy said
sourly, swaying on his feet.

"There's only one kind of money," Fenn said. "Just as there's only one
kind of law, even though there's different kinds of men enforcing it." He
looked at me as I came up. "Much obliged, son."

"*Por nada*," I said. "You get in certain habits when you've had a badge in
the family. My daddy was sheriff here once."

"So? I didn't know that." Fenn looked at me sharply. "Don't look like
you're making any plans to follow in his footsteps. That's hardly a lawman's
rig you're wearing."

I said, "Maybe, but I never yet beat a man over the head while I was shaking his hand, Marshal."

"Son," he said, "my job is to enforce the law and maybe make a small profit on the side, not to play games with fair and unfair." He looked at me for a moment longer. "Well, maybe we'll meet again. It depends."

"On what?" I asked.

"On the price," he said. "The price on your head."

"But I haven't got—"

"Not now," he said. "But you will, wearing those guns. I know the signs. I've seen them before, too many times. Don't count on having me under obligation to you, when your time comes. I never let personal feelings interfere with business. . . . Easy, now," he said, to a couple of fellows who were lifting LeBaron, bound hand and foot, into the wagon that somebody had driven up. "Easy. Don't damage the merchandise. I take pride in delivering them in good shape for standing trial, whenever possible."

I decided I needed a drink, and then I changed my mind in favor of a cup of coffee. As I walked down the street, leaving my pony at the rail back there, the wagon rolled past and went out of town ahead of me. I was still watching it, for no special reason, when Waco stepped from the alley behind me.

"Jim!" he said. "Turn around, Jim!"

I turned slowly. He was a little unsteady on his feet, standing there, maybe from my hitting him, maybe from drinking. I thought it was drinking. I hadn't hit him very hard. He'd had time for a couple of quick ones, and liquor always got to him fast.

"You sold us out, you damn traitor!" he cried. "You took sides with the law!"

"I never was against it," I said. "Not really."

"After everything I've done for you!" he said thickly. "I was going to make you a great man, Jim, greater than Longley or Hardin or Hickok or any of them. With my brains and your size and speed, nothing could have stopped us! But you turned on me! Do you think you can do it alone? Is that what you're figuring, to leave me behind now that I've built you up to be somebody?"

"Waco," I said, "I never had any ambitions to be—"

"You and your medicine guns!" he sneered. "Let me tell you something. Those old guns are just something I picked up in a pawnshop. I spun a good yarn about them to give you confidence. You were on the edge, you needed a push in the right direction, and I knew once you started wearing a flashy rig like that, with one killing under your belt already, somebody'd be bound to try you again, and we'd be on our way to fame. But as for their being Bill Longley's guns, don't make me laugh!"

I said, "Waco—"

"They's just metal and wood like any other guns!" he said. "And I'm going to prove it to you right now! I don't need you, Jim! I'm as good a man as you, even if you laugh at me and make jokes at my expense. . . . *Are you ready, Jim?*"

He was crouching, and I looked at him, Waco Smith, with whom I'd ridden up the trail and back. I saw that he was no good and I saw that he was dead. It didn't matter whose guns I was wearing, and all he'd really said was that he didn't know whose guns they were. But it didn't matter, they were my guns now, and he was just a little runt who never could shoot for shucks, anyway. He was dead, and so were the others, the ones who'd come after him, because they'd come, I knew that.

I saw them come to try me, one after the other, and I saw them go down before the big black guns, all except the last, the one I couldn't quite make out. Maybe it was Fenn and maybe it wasn't. . . .

I said, "To hell with you, Waco. I've got nothing against you, and I'm not going to fight you. Tonight or any other time."

I turned and walked away. I heard the sound of his gun behind me an instant before the bullet hit me. Then I wasn't hearing anything for a while. When I came to, I was in bed, and Martha Butcher was there.

"Jim!" she breathed. "Oh, Jim. . . !"

She looked real worried, and kind of pretty, I thought, but of course I was half out of my head. She looked even prettier the day I asked her to marry me, some months later, but maybe I was a little out of my head that day, too. Old Man Butcher didn't like it a bit. It seems his fight with Martha had been about her cleaning up my place, and his ordering her to quit and stay away from that young troublemaker, as he'd called me after getting word of all the hell we'd raised up north after delivering his cattle.

He didn't like it, but he offered me a job, I suppose for Martha's sake. I thanked him and told him I was much obliged but I'd just accepted an appointment as Deputy U.S. Marshal. Seems like somebody had recommended me for the job, maybe Old Joe Fenn, maybe not. I got my old gun out of my bedroll and wore it tucked inside my belt when I thought I might need it. It was a funny thing how seldom I had any use for it, even wearing a badge. With that job, I was the first in the neighborhood to hear about Waco Smith. The news came from New Mexico Territory. Waco and a bunch had pulled a job over there, and a posse had trapped them in a box canyon and shot them to pieces.

I never wore the other guns again. After we moved into the old place, I hung them on the wall. It was right after I'd run against Billy Bates for sheriff and won that I came home to find them gone. Martha looked surprised when I asked about them.

"Why," she said, "I gave them to your friend, Mr. Williams. He said you'd sold them to him. Here's the money."

I counted the money, and it was a fair enough price for a pair of second-hand guns and holsters, but I hadn't met any Mr. Williams.

I started to say so, but Martha was still talking. She said, "He certainly had an odd first name, didn't he? Who'd christen anybody Long Williams? Not that he wasn't big enough. I guess he'd be as tall as you, wouldn't he, if he didn't have that trouble with his neck?"

"His neck?" I said.

"Why, yes," she said. "Didn't you notice when you talked to him, the way he kept his head cocked to the side? Like this."

She showed me how Long Williams had kept his head cocked to the side. She looked real pretty doing it, and I couldn't figure how I'd ever thought her plain, but maybe she'd changed. Or maybe I had. I kissed her and gave her back the gun money to buy something for herself, and went outside to think. Long Williams, William Longley. A man with a wry neck and a man who was hanged twice. It was kind of strange, to be sure, but after a time I decided it was just a coincidence. Some drifter riding by just saw the guns through the window and took a fancy to them.

I mean, if it had really been Bill Longley, if he was alive and had his guns back, we'd surely have heard of him by now down at the sheriff's office, and we never have.

The Hanging That Didn't Take

This story opens with a scene that recalls Andy Adams's *The Log of a Cowboy*. A young drover, going up the trail for the first time, kills a man in Dodge City. One night, while the cowboys are on the trail going home, a blanket is spread on the ground for a card game. It is there that the kid first hears the legend of a famous Texas gunfighter.

William Longley was no legend: he was real. He was a tall boy, almost a "giant" even by Texas standards, when he killed his first man at the age of fifteen. By age twenty-seven, when he was executed by hanging, he claimed to have killed thirty-two. Waco's yarn about Longley surviving the rope after being hung as a horsethief probably originated after Longley's execution in 1878 at Giddings, Texas. The events there were a bit out of the ordinary.

The rope slipped, two separate sources say, and Bill Longley was so tall that his feet hit the ground before his neck snapped. So some spectators—or some deputies—lifted him up while the rope was shortened. Then he was hung again until he was dead.

Or was he? For years afterward, rumors circulated that a sort of harness had been smuggled to Longley, a harness that prevented the noose from breaking his neck. The friends who buried him outside the cemetery, according to the stories, had actually buried an empty coffin. And Longley was never heard from again.

In one sense Hamilton's "The Guns of William Longley" is a ghost story. However, Longley is not the ghost: the men in the story are haunted by something else, by a way of life that died in the Civil War.

After Gettysburg and Appomattox, many Confederate soldiers had nothing to go home to. They had lived by the gun, exempt from any law except that of the military, and they had fought, they claimed, for the honor of the South. Gangs of them rode out into the Kansas and Texas territory after the war and went on trying to live by the old code of the South. They were the kind of men who would defend their honor by dueling in the old-fashioned manner.

Mr. Carmichael and Jim Anderson both fit this pattern. They call each other "sir"; one issues a challenge and the other accepts it; the man who has the clear advantage allows the other man the first shot—in this case, the first two shots. Rather than a gunfight, this is a duel.

Shooting Carmichael is what turns Jim around, enabling him to resist the temptation to join the outlaw gang of Dutch LeBaron. "I was fighting the Longley gun for Mr. Carmichael's life," Jim says. And he wins. He no longer sees the justification in lawlessness, or even in duels.

Was it William Longley, somehow still alive, who returned for his guns? Or was it some evil spirit, come to take away the pistols so that they could be used to tempt another young lawless hell-raiser?

William Eastlake

b. 1917

Born in Brooklyn and raised in New Jersey, William Eastlake experienced a meta-morphosis when he purchased a cattle ranch in New Mexico and began to write about the Southwest. He became a natural Westerner.

Before this transformation, Eastlake fought in the trenches of France and Belgium during World War II and was wounded in the Battle of the Bulge in 1944. After 1950 he began spending time at a brother-in-law's ranch in the Jemez Mountains of New Mexico. It was there that he found the people, the cultures, and the conflicts, along with the beauty and harshness of the landscape, that were to figure significantly in his fiction.

Eastlake has earned a good reputation for himself through his novels, which include *Go in Beauty, Dances in the Scalp House, Portrait of an Artist with Twenty-six Horses,* and *The Bronc People*. Fellow author and critic Gerald Haslam states emphatically that "William Eastlake is a consummate short story writer, a great one." His ability to work well in both forms of fiction might explain why so many of his short stories (including "The Death of Sun") have also appeared as episodes in his novels.

The Death of Sun

The bird Sun was named Sun by the Indians because each day their final eagle circled this part of the reservation like the clock of sun. Sun, a grave and golden eagle-stream of light, sailed without movement as though propelled by some eternity, to orbit, to circumnavigate this moon of earth, to alight upon his aerie from which he had risen, and so Sun would sit with the same God dignity and decorous finality with which he had emerged—then once more without seeming volition ride the crest of an updraft above Indian Country on six-foot wings to settle again on this throne aerie in awful splendor, admonitory, serene—regal and doomed. I have risen.

"'Man,' Feodor Dostoevski said," the white teacher Mary-Forge said, "'without a sure idea of himself and the purpose of his life cannot live and would sooner destroy himself than remain on earth.'"

"Who was Dostoevski?" the Navajo Indian Jesus Saves said.

"An Indian."

"What kind?"

"With that comment he could have been a Navajo," Mary-Forge said.

"No way," Jesus Saves said.

"Why, no way could Dostoevski be an Indian?"

"I didn't say Dostoevski couldn't be an Indian; I said he couldn't be a Navajo."

"Why is a Navajo different?"

"We are, that's all," Jesus Saves said. "In the words of Sören Kierkegaard—"

"Who was Sören Kierkegaard?"

"Another Russian," Jesus Saves said.

"Kierkegaard was a Dane."

"No, that was Hamlet," Jesus Saves said. "Remember?"

"You're peeved, Jesus Saves."

"No, I'm bugged," Jesus Saves said, "by people who start sentences with 'man.'"

"Dostoevski was accounting for the high suicide rate among Navajos. Since the white man invaded Navajo country the Navajo sees no hope or purpose to life."

"Then why didn't Dostoevski say that?"

"Because he never heard of the Navajo."

"Then I never heard of Dostoevski," Bull Who Looks Up said. "Two can play at this game."

"That's right," Jesus Saves said, sure of himself now and with purpose.

"What is the purpose of your life, Jesus Saves?"

"To get out of this school," Jesus Saves said.

Jesus Saves was named after a signboard erected by the Albuquerque First National Savings & Loan.

All of Mary-Forge's students were Navajos. When Mary-Forge was not ranching she was running this free school that taught the Indians about themselves and their country—Indian country.

"What has Dostoevski got to do with Indian country?"

"I'm getting to that," Mary-Forge said.

"Will you hurry up?"

"No," Mary-Forge said.

"Is that any way for a teacher to speak to a poor Indian?"

"Sigmund Freud," the Medicine Man said, "said—more in anguish I believe than in criticism—'What does the Indian want? My God, what does the Indian want?'"

"He said that about women."

"If he had lived longer, he would have said it about Indians."

"True."

"Why?"

"Because it sounds good, it sounds profound, it tends to make you take off and beat the hell out of the Indians."

"After we have finished off the women."

"The women were finished off a long time ago," the Medicine Man said.

"But like the Indians they can make a comeback."

"Who knows," the Medicine Man said, "we both may be a dying race."

"Who knows?"

"We both may have reached the point of no return, who knows?"

"If we don't want to find out, what the hell are we doing in school?"

"Who knows?"

"I know," Mary-Forge said, "I know all about the eagle."

"Tell us, Mary-Forge, all about the eagle."

"The eagle is being killed off."

"We know that; what do we do?"

"We get out of this school and find the people who are killing the eagle."

"Then?"

"Who knows?" Mary-Forge said.

Mary-Forge was a young woman—she was the youngest white woman the Navajos had ever seen. She was not a young girl, there are millions of young girls in America. In America young white girls suddenly become defeated women. A young white woman sure of herself and with a purpose in life such as Mary-Forge was unknown to the American Indian.

Mary-Forge had large, wide-apart, almond-shaped eyes, high full cheekbones, cocky let-us-all-give-thanks tipsy breasts, and good brains. The white American man is frightened by her brain. The Indian found it nice. They loved it. They tried to help Mary-Forge. Mary-Forge tried to help the Indians. They were both cripples. Both surrounded by the white reservation.

High on her right cheekbone Mary-Forge had a jagged two-inch scar caused by a stomping she got from high-heeled cowboy boots belonging to a sheep rancher from the Twin Slash Heart Ranch on the floor of the High Point Bar in Gallup.

Mary-Forge did not abruptly think of eagles in the little red schoolhouse filled with Indians. A helicopter had just flown over. The helicopter came to kill eagles. The only time the Indians ever saw or felt a helicopter on the red reservation was when the white ranchers came to kill eagles. Eagles killed sheep, they said, and several cases have been known, they said, where white babies have been plucked from playpens and dropped in the ocean, they said.

You could hear plainly the *whack-whack-whack* of the huge rotor blades of the copter in the red schoolhouse. The yellow and blue copter was being flown by a flat-faced doctor-serious white rancher named Ira Osmun, who believed in conservation through predator control. Eagles were fine birds, but the sheep must be protected. Babies, too.

"Mr. Osmun," Wilson Drago, the shotgun-bearing sado-child-appearing copilot asked, "have the eagles got any white babies lately?"

"No."

"Then?"

"Because we are exercising predator control."

"When was the last white baby snatched by eagles and dropped into the ocean?"

"Not eagles, Drago, eagle; it only takes one. As long as there is one eagle there is always the possibility of your losing your child."

"I haven't any child."

"If you did."

"But I haven't."

"Someone does."

"No one in the area does."

"If they did, there would be the possibility of their losing them."

"No one can say nay to that," Wilson Drago said. "When was the last time a child was snatched?"

"It must have been a long time ago."

"Before living memory?"

"Yes, even then, Drago, I believe the stories to be apocryphal."

"What's that mean?"

"Lies."

"Then why are we shooting the eagles?"

"Because city people don't care about sheep. City people care about babies. You tell the people in Albuquerque that their babies have an outside chance, any chance that their baby will be snatched up and the possibility that it will be dropped in the ocean, kerplunk, and they will let you kill eagles."

"How far is the ocean?"

"People don't care how far the ocean is; they care about their babies."

"True."

"It's that simple."

"When was the last lamb that was snatched up?"

"Yesterday."

"That's serious."

"You better believe it, Drago."

"Why are we hovering over this red hogan?"

"Because before we kill an eagle we got to make sure what Mary-Forge is up to."

"What was she up to last time you heard?"

"Shooting down helicopters."

"All by herself?"

"It only takes one shot."

"You know, I bet that's right."

"You better believe it, Drago."

"Is this where she lives?"

"No—this is the little red schoolhouse she uses to get the Indians to attack the whites."

"What happened to your other copilots?"

"They got scared and quit."

"The last one?"

"Scared and quit."

"Just because of one woman?"

"Yes. You're not scared of a woman, are you, Drago?"

"No, I mean yes."

"Which is it, yes or no?"

"Yes," Wilson Drago said.

Below in the red hogan that was shaped like a beehive with a hole on top for the smoke to come out, the Indians and Mary-Forge were getting ready to die on the spot.

"I'm not getting ready to die on the spot," Bull Who Looks Up said.

"You want to save the eagles, don't you?" Mary-Forge said.

"Let me think about that," Jesus Saves said.

"Pass me the gun," Mary-Forge said.

Now, from above in the copter the hogan below looked like a gun turret, a small fort defending the perimeter of Indian Country.

"Mary-Forge is an interesting problem," Ira Osmun said—shouted—above the *whack-whack-whack* of the rotors.

"Every woman is."

"But every woman doesn't end up living with the Indians, with the eagles."

"What causes that?"

"We believe the Indians and the eagles become their surrogate children."

"That they become a substitute for life."

"Oh? Why do you hate me?"

"What?"

"Why do you use such big words?"

"I'm sorry, Drago. Do you see any eagles?"

"No, but I see a gun."

"Where?"

"Coming out the top of the hogan."

"Let Mary-Forge fire first."

"Why?"

"To establish a point of law. Then it's not between her eagles and my sheep."

"It becomes your ass or hers."

"Yes."

"But it could be my life."

"I've considered that, Drago."

"Thank you. Thank you very much," Wilson Drago said.

Sun, the golden eagle that was very carefully watching the two white animals that lived in the giant bird that went *whack-whack-whack*, was ready.

Today would be the day of death for Sun. His mate had been killed two days before. Without her the eaglets in the woven of yucca high basket nest would die. Today would be the day of death for Sun because, without a sure idea of himself, without purpose in life, an eagle would sooner destroy himself than remain on earth. The last day of Sun.

"Because," Mary-Forge said, and taking the weapon and jerking in a shell, "because I know, even though the Indians and us and the eagle, even though we have no chance ever, we can go through the motions of courage, compassion, and concern. Because we are Sun and men, too. Hello, Sun."

"Stop talking and aim carefully."

"Did I say something?"

"You made a speech."

"I'm sorry," Mary-Forge said.

"Aim carefully."

Mary-Forge was standing on the wide shoulders of an Indian named When Someone Dies He Is Remembered. All the other Indians who belonged in the little red schoolhouse stood around and below her in the dim and alive dust watching Mary-Forge revolve like a gun turret with her lever-operated Marlin .30-30 pointing out of the smoke hatch high up on the slow-turning and hard shoulders of When Someone Dies He Is Remembered.

"Why don't you shoot?" More Turquoise said. He almost whispered it, as though the great noise of the copter did not exist.

"The thing keeps bobbing," Mary-Forge shouted down to the Indians.

Looking through the gunsights she had to go up and down up and down to try and get a shot. She did not want to hit the cowboys. It would be good enough to hit the engine or the rotor blades. Why not hit the cowboys? Because there are always more cowboys. There are not many eagles left on the planet earth, there are several million cowboys. There are more cowboys than there are Indians. That's for sure. But what is important now is that if we give one eagle for one cowboy soon all the eagles will have disappeared from the earth and the cowboys will be standing in your bed. No, the helicopter is scarce. They will not give one helicopter for one eagle. A helicopter costs too much money. How much? A quarter-million dollars, I bet. Hit them where their heart is. Hit them right in their helicopter.

But it danced. Now Mary-Forge noticed that although it was dancing it was going up and down with a rhythm. The thing to do is to wait until it hits bottom and then follow it up. She did and fired off a shot.

"Good girl," the Medicine Man said.

"That was close," Ira Osmun said to his shotgun, Wilson Drago. "Now that we know where Mary-Forge is we can chase the eagle."

Ira Osmun allowed the chopper to spurt up and away to tilt off at a weird angle so that it clawed its way sideways like a crab that flew, a piece of junk, of tin and chrome and gaudy paint, alien and obscene in the perfect pure blue New Mexican sky, an intruder in the path of sun. Now the chopper clawed its way to the aerie of Sun.

The eagle had watched it all happen. Sun had watched it happen many times now. Two days ago when they killed his mate was the last time. Sun looked down at his golden eagle chicks. The eaglets were absolute white, they would remain white and vulnerable for several months until the new feathers. But there was no more time. Sun watched the huge man junk bird clawing its way down the long valley that led to Mount Taylor. His home, his home and above all the homes of the Indians.

Like the Indians, the ancestors of Sun had one time roamed a virgin continent abloom with the glory of life, alive with fresh flashing streams, a smogless sky, all the world a sweet poem of life where all was beginning. Nothing ever ended. Now it was all ending. The eagle, Sun, did not prepare to defend himself. He would not defend himself. There was nothing now to defend. The last hour of Sun.

"Catch me," Mary-Forge shouted from the top of the hogan, and jumped. When she was caught by More Turquoise, she continued to shout, as the noise of the chopper was still there. "They've taken off for Mount Taylor to kill Sun. We've got to get on our horses and get our ass over there."

"Why?"

"To save Sun," Mary-Forge shouted. "Sun is the last eagle left in the county."

"But this is not a movie," the Medicine Man said. "We don't have to get on horses and gallop across the prairie. We can get in my pickup and drive there—quietly."

"On the road it will take two hours," Mary-Forge said. "And we'll need horses when we get there to follow the chopper."

"What would Dostoevski say about this?" the Medicine Man said.

"To hell with Dostoevski," Mary-Forge said.

Outside they slammed the saddles on the amazed Indian ponies, then threw themselves on and fled down the canyon, a stream of dust and light, a commingling of vivid flash and twirl so when they disappeared into the cottonwoods you held your breath until the phantoms, the abrupt magic of motion, appeared again on the Cabrillo draw.

"Come on now, baby," Mary-Forge whispered to her horse Poco Mas. "What I said about Dostoevski I didn't mean. Poor Dostoevski. I meant seconds count. We didn't have time for a philosophical discussion. Come on now, baby, move good. Be good to me, baby, move good. Move good, baby. Move good. You can take that fence, baby. Take him! Good boy, baby. Good boy, Poco. Good boy. I'm sure the Medicine Man understands that when there are so few left, so few left Poco that there is not time for niceties. You'd think an Indian would understand that, wouldn't you? Still Medicine Man is a strange Indian. A Freudian Medicine Man. But Bull Who Looks Up understands, look at him go. He's pulling ahead of us are you going to let him get away with that Poco?" Poco did not let the horse of Bull Who Looks Up stay ahead but passed him quickly, with Mary-Forge swinging her gun high and Bull Who Looks Up gesturing with his gun at the tin bird that crabbed across the sky.

"You see, Drago," Ira Osmun shouted to Wilson Drago, "we are the villains of the piece."

"What?"

"The bad guys."

"It's pretty hard to think of yourself as the bad guy, Mr. Osmun."

"Well, we are."

"Who are the good guys?"

"Mary-Forge."

"Screw me."

"No, she wouldn't do that because you're a bad guy. Because you kill eagles. People who never saw an eagle, never will see an eagle, never want to see an eagle, want eagles all over the place. Except the poor. The poor want sheep to eat. Did you ever hear of a poor person complaining about the lack of eagles? They have got an outfit of rich gentlemen called the Sierra Club. They egg on Indian-lovers like Mary-Forge to kill ranchers."

"Why?"

"They have nothing else to do."

"You think Mary-Forge actually has sex with the Indians?"

"Why else would she be on the reservation?"

"I never thought about that."

"Think about it."

"I guess you're right."

"Drago, what do you think about?"

"I don't think about eagles."

"What do you think about?"

"Ordinarily?"

"Yes."

"Like when I'm drinking?"

"Yes."

"Religion."

"Good, Drago, I like to hear you say that. Good. What religion?"

"They are all good. I guess Billy Graham is the best."

"Yes, if you're stupid."

"What?"

"Nothing, Drago. Keep your eye peeled for the eagle."

"You said I was stupid."

"I may have said the Sierra Club was stupid."

"Did you?"

"No, how could you be stupid and be that rich?"

"Why are they queer for eagles then?"

"They are for anything that is getting scarce. Indians, eagles, anything. Mary-Forge is against natural evolution, too."

"What's natural evolution mean?"

"When something is finished it's finished, forget it. We got a new evolution, the machine, this copter, a new bird."

"That makes sense."

"Remember we don't want to kill eagles."

"We have to."

"That's right."

The eagle that had to be killed, Sun, perched like an eagle on his aerie throne. A king, a keeper of one hundred square miles of Indian Country, an arbiter, a jury and judge, a shadow clock that had measured time for two thousand years in slow shadow circle and so now the earth, the Indians, the place, would be without reckoning, certainly without the serene majesty of Sun, without, and this is what is our epitaph and harbinger, without the gold of silence the long lonely shadow beneath silent wing replaced now by the *whack-whack-whack* of tin, proceeding with crablike crippled claw—the sweet song of man in awkward crazy metallic and cockeyed pounce, approached Sun.

Sun looked down on the eaglets in the nest. The thing to do would be to glide away from the whack-bird away from the nest. To fight it out somewhere else. If he could tangle himself in the wings of the whack-bird, that would be the end of whack-bird. The end of Sun. Sun jumped off his aerie without movement, not abrupt or even peremptory but as though the reel of film had cut, and then proceeded to a different scene. The bird Sun, the eagle, the great golden glider moving across the wilds of purple mesa in air-fed steady no-beat, in hushed deadly amaze, seemed in funeral stateliness, mounting upward on invisible winds toward the other sun.

"If he climbs, we will climb with him, Drago. He is bound to run out of updrafts."

Wilson Drago slid open the door on his side and shifted the Harrington & Richardson pump gun into the ready position.

"How high will this thing climb, sir?"

"Ten thousand feet."

"The bird can climb higher than that."

"Yet he has to come down, Drago."

"How much fuel we got?"

"Fifty gallons."

"What are we consuming?"

"A gallon a minute."

"Shall I try a shot?"

"Yes."

Sun was spiraling upward in tight circles on a good rising current of air when the pellets of lead hit him. They hit like a gentle rain that gave him a quick lift. Sun was out of range. Both the copter and Sun were spiraling upward. The copter was gaining.

"Shall I try another shot?"

"Yes."

This time the lead pellets slammed into Sun like a hard rain and shoved him upward and crazy tilted him as a great ship will yaw in a sudden gust. Sun was still out of range.

Now the upward current of air ceased, collapsed under Sun abruptly and the copter closed the distance until Ira Osmun and Wilson Drago were alongside and looking into small yellow eyes as the great sailing ship of Sun coasted downward into deep sky.

"Shall I try a shot?"

"Yes."

Wilson Drago raised the Harrington & Richardson shotgun and pumped in a shell with a solid slam. He could almost touch Sun with the muzzle. The swift vessel of Sun sailed on as though expecting to take the broadside from the 12-gauge gun that would send him to the bottom—to the floor of earth.

"Now, Drago."

But the gliding ship of bird had already disappeared—folded its huge wing of sail and shot downward, down down down downward until just before earth it unleashed its enormous sail of wing and glided over the surface of earth—Indian Country. Down came the copter in quick chase.

There stood the Indians all in a row.

"Don't fire, men," Mary-Forge shouted, "until Sun has passed."

As Sun sailed toward the Indians the shadow of Sun came first, shading each Indian separately. Now came the swifting Sun and each mounted Indian raised his gun in salute. Again separately and in the order which Sun arrived and passed, now the Indians leveled their guns to kill the whack-bird.

"Oh, this is great, Drago," Ira Osmun shouted, "the Indians want to fight."

"What's great about that?"

"It's natural to fight Indians."

"It is?"

"Yes."

"Well, I'll be."

"My grandfather would be proud of us now."

"Did he fight Indians?"

"He sure did. It's only a small part of the time the whites have been that they haven't fought Indians."

"Fighting has been hard on the Indians."

"That may well be, Drago, but it's natural."

"Why?"

"Because people naturally have a fear of strangers. It's called xenophobia. When you don't go along with nature you get into trouble. You suppress your natural instincts and that is dangerous. That's what's wrong with this country."

"It is? I wondered about that."

"There's nothing wrong with shooting Indians."

"I wondered about that."

"It's natural."

"No, Mr. Osmun there is something wrong."

"What's that?"

"Look. The Indians are shooting back."

Ira Osmun twisted the copter up and away. "Get out the rifle. We'll take care of the Indians."

"What about the eagle?"

"We've first got to take care of the Indians who are shooting at us and that girl who is shooting at us."

"Is she crazy?"

"Why else would she have intercourse with the Indians?"

"You mean screwing them?"

"Yes."

"She could have all sorts of reasons. We don't even know that she is screwing them. Maybe we are screwing the Indians."

"Drago, we discussed this before and decided that Mary-Forge was."

"What if she is?"

"Drago, you can't make up your mind about anything. You're being neurotic. When you don't understand why you do something you're being neurotic."

"I am?"

"Yes, get out the rifle."

"I still think it's her business if she is queer for Indians and eagles."

"But not if she shoots at us when she's doing it; that's neurotic."

"You're right there, Mr. Osmun."

"Get the rifle."

"O.K."

"You know, Drago, people, particularly people who love the Indians, are suppressing a need to kill them. It's called a love-hate relationship."

"It is? You can stop talk now, Mr. Osmun. I said I'd get the rifle."

Below the helicopter that circled in the brilliant, eye-hurting, New Mexican day, Mary-Forge told the Indians that the copter would be back, that the ranchers would not fight the eagle while being fired on by Indians. "The ranchers will not make the same mistake Custer did."

"What was that?"

"Fight on two fronts. Custer attacked the Sioux before he finished off Sitting Bull. We are the Sioux."

"We are? That's nice," the Navajo Bull Who Looks Up said. "When do we get out of this class?"

"We never do," Jesus Saves said.

"Get your ass behind the rocks!" the teacher Mary-Forge shouted. "Here they come!"

The copter flew over and sprayed the rocks with M-16 automatic rifle fire.

"That should teach the teacher that we outgun them, Drago," Ira Osmun said. "Now we can get the eagle!"

The golden eagle called Sun spiraled upward again, its wings steady, wild, sure, in the glorious and rapt quietude of the blue, blue, blue New Mexico morning, a golden eagle against the blue, a kind of heliograph, and a flashing jewel in the perfect and New Mexico sea of sky. The gold eagle, recapitulent, lost then found as it twirled steady and upward in the shattered light, followed by the tin bird.

Sun knew that he must gain height. All the power of maneuver lay in getting above the tin bird. He knew, too, and from experience that the tin bird could only go a certain height. He knew, too, and from experience that the air current he rode up could collapse at once and without warning. He knew, too, and from the experience of several battles now with the bird of tin that the enemy was quick and could spit things out that could pain then kill. All this he knew from experience. But the tin bird was learning, too.

The tin bird jerked upward after the golden eagle. The golden eagle, Sun, wandered upward as though searching and lost. A last and final tryst in the list of Indian Country because now always until now, until now no one killed everything that moved. You always had a chance. Now there was no chance. Soon there would be no Sun.

"Remember, Drago, I've got to stay away from him or above him—he can take us with him. The last time when we got his mate he almost took us with him; I just barely got away when he attacked the rotors—when the rotor goes we go, Drago—we fall like a rock, smash like glass. They will pick you up with a dustpan."

"Who?"

"Those Indians down there."

"Mr. Osmun, I don't want to play this game."

"You want to save the sheep, don't you?"

"No."

"Why not?"

"I don't have any sheep to save."

"You don't have any sheep, you don't have any children. But you have pride."

"I don't know."

"Then fire when I tell you to and you'll get some."

"I don't know."

"Do you want eagles to take over the country?"

"I don't know."

"Eagles and Indians at one time controlled this whole country, Drago; you couldn't put out a baby or a lamb in my grandfather's time without an Indian or an eagle would grab it. Now we got progress. Civilization. That means a man is free to go about his business."

"It does?"

"Yes, now that we got them on those ropes we can't let them go, Drago."

"We can't?"

"No, that would be letting civilized people down. It would be letting my grandfather down. What would I say to him?"

"Are you going to see your grandfather?"

"No, he's dead. We'll be dead, too, Drago, if you don't shoot. That eagle will put us down there so those Indians will pick us up with a dustpan. You don't want that, do you?"

"I don't know."

"You better find out right smart or I'll throw you out of this whack-bird myself."

"Would you?"

"Someone's got to live, Drago. The eagle doesn't want to live."

"Why do you say that?"

"He knew we were after him. He knew we would get him; he could have left the country. He could have flown north to Canada. He would be protected there."

"Maybe he thinks this is his country."

"No, this is civilized country. Will you shoot the eagle?"

"No."

"I like the eagle and the Indians as well as the next man, Drago, but we have to take sides. It's either my sheep or them. Whose side are you on, Drago?"

"I guess I'm on theirs."

The helicopter was much lighter now without Drago in it. The copter handled much better and was able to gain on the eagle.

Ira Osmun continued to talk to Wilson Drago as though he were still there. Wilson Drago was one of Ira Osmun's sheepherders and should have taken a more active interest in sheep.

"The way I see it, Drago, if you wouldn't defend me, the eagle would have brought us both down. It was only a small push I gave you, almost a touch as you were leaning out. By lightening the plane you made a small contribution to civilization.

"We all do what we can, Drago, and you have contributed your bit. If there is anything I can't stand, it's an enemy among my sheep."

The copter continued to follow the eagle up but now more lightsome and quick with more alacrity and interest in the chase.

The Indians on the ground were amazed to see the white man come down. Another dropout. "Poor old Wilson Drago. We knew him well. Another man who couldn't take progress—civilization. Many times has Drago shot at us while we were stealing his sheep. We thought anyone might be a dropout but not Wilson Drago. It shows you how tough it's getting on the white reservation. They're killing each other. Soon there will be nothing left but Indians."

"Good morning, Indian."

"Good morning, Indian."

"Isn't it a beautiful day. Do you notice there is nothing left but us Indians?"

"And one eagle."

The Indians were making all these strange observations over what remained of the body of the world's leading sheepherder, Wilson Drago.

"He created quite a splash."

"And I never thought he would make it."

"The last time I saw him drunk in Gallup I thought he was coming apart, but this is a surprise."

"I knew he had it in him, but I never expected it to come out all at once."

"I can't find his scalp. What do you suppose he did with it? Did he hide it?"

"The other white man got it."

"I bet he did."

"They don't care about Indians anymore."

"No, when they drop in on you they don't bring their scalp."

"Please, please," Mary-Forge said, "the man is dead."

"Man? Man? I don't see any man, just a lot of blood and shit."

"Well, there is a man, or was a man."

"Well, there's nothing now," Bull Who Looks Up said, "not even a goddamn scalp."

"Well, Drago's in the white man's heaven," More Turquoise said. "On streets of gold tending his flock."

"And shooting eagles."

"Drago's going higher and higher to white man's heaven, much higher than his what-do-you-call-it—"

"Helicopter."

"—can go," Jesus Saves said.

"I don't like all this sacrilege," Mary-Forge said. "Remember I am a Christian."

"What?"

"I was brought up in the Christian tradition."

"Now you're hedging," When Someone Dies He Is Remembered said.

Ah, these Indians, Mary-Forge thought, how did I get involved? And she said aloud, "Once upon a time I was young and innocent."

"Print that!" Bull Who Looks Up said.

"We better get higher on the mountain," Mary-Forge shouted at the Indians, "so when Osmun closes on the eagle we can get a better shot."

"O.K., Teacher."

"There's only one white guy left," she said.

"I find that encouraging if true," More Turquoise said.

"Load your rifles and pull your horses after you," Mary-Forge said.

"My Country 'Tis of Thee," Ira Osmun hummed as he swirled the copter in pursuit of the eagle. You didn't die in vain, Drago. That is, you were not vain, you were a very modest chap. We can climb much higher without you, Drago. I am going to get the last eagle this time, Drago. I think he's reached the top of his climb.

Sun watched the tin whack-bird come up. The tin bird came up *whack-whack-whack*, its wings never flapping just turning in a big circle. What did it eat? How did it mate? Where did it come from? From across the huge water on a strong wind. The evil wind. Sun circled seeing that he must get higher, the tin bird was coming up quicker today. Sun could see the people he always saw below. The people who lived in his country, filing up the mountain. They seemed to be wanting to get closer to him now.

Ira Osmun felt then saw all the Indians in the world firing at him from below. How are you going to knock down an eagle when all the Indians in the world are firing at you from Mount Taylor? It was Mary-Forge who put them up to it, for sure. An Indian would not have the nerve to shoot at a white man. You don't have to drop down and kill all the Indians. They—the people in the East—who have no sheep would call that a massacre. Indians are very popular at the moment. If you simply knock off Mary-Forge, that would do the trick. Women are not very popular at the moment. Why? Because they have a conspiracy against men. You didn't know that? It's true, Drago. The woman used to be happy to be on the bottom. Now she wants to be on the top.

No?

Did you say something, Drago?

I thought I heard someone say something. I must have been hit. My mind must be wandering. What was I saying? It's part of the conspiracy. What's that mean? Something. I must have been hit. What was I doing? Oh yes, I was going to get Mary-Forge—the girl who is queer for Indians and eagles. The eagle can wait.

And Ira Osmun put the copter in full throttle, then cradled the M-16 automatic rifle on his left arm with muzzle pointing out the door. With his right hand he placed the copter in a swift power glide down.

Sun saw the obscene tin bird go into its dive down. Now would be a chance to get it while the tin bird was busy hunting its prey on the ground. Sun took one more final look over the aerie nest to check the birds. The eaglets were doing fine. Drawing the enemy away from the nest had been successful. The eaglets craned their necks at the familiar shape before Sun folded his great span of wings and shot down on top of the tin bird.

Mary-Forge mounted on Poco Mas saw the tin bird coming, the M-16 quicking out nicks of flame. She could not get the Indians to take cover. The Indians had placed their horses behind the protection of the boulders and were all standing out in the open and were blasting away at the zooming-in copter. Mary-Forge was still shouting at the Indians, but they would not take cover. They have seen too many goddamn movies, Mary-Forge thought, they have read too many books. They are stupid, stupid, stupid, dumb, dumb, dumb Indians. How stupid and how dumb can you get? They want to save the eagle. Standing exposed naked to the machine gun. The stupid Indians. Mary-Forge raised her rifle at the zooming-in copter in a follow-me gesture, then took off in a straight line, the horse pounding, and the flame-nicking copter followed, so did Sun. So now there were three.

The tin bird was alive in flame all at once, something had hit the fuel tank and all of everything exploded in fire, the rotors of the tin bird were still turning and fanning the flame so that it was not only a streaking meteor across Indian Country but at once a boil of fire that shot downward from the terrific draft laying a torch of flame across the desert so that the mesquite and sagebrush became a steady line of flame ending where the tin whack-bird hit into the rocks and went silent in a grand tower of fire.

"It was Sun that did it," More Turquoise said.

The death of Sun.

All of the Indians and Mary-Forge were standing around the dying fire of the big whack-bird in the smoke that shrouded the death of Sun.

"When an eagle," the Medicine Man said, "—when a true bird has no hope—"

"Yes?"

"When the eagle is no more," the Medicine Man said.

"Yes?"

"Then we are no more."

"Yes," every person shrouded in smoke said.

Look up there. It was within three months when When Someone Dies He Is Remembered remembered that an eagle named Star by Medicine Man sailed in one beginning night to reclaim the country of Sun. Now Star's wide shadow passed over the dead tin whack-bird then he, the great eagle Star, settled on his throne aerie in awful and mimic splendor, and again admonitory, serene—regal and doomed?

A Shootout in the Sky

The shootout in "The Death of Sun" is like that old B-Western movie scene where the Indians have surrounded a Conestoga wagon or a homesteader's cabin and are riding around in circles shooting when suddenly over the hill comes a troop of U.S. Cavalry to the rescue. Only in Eastlake's story, two white guys in a helicopter are flying around a lone eagle, shooting, and the Indians come riding to the rescue.

"We are exercising predator control," says the white rancher who flies the helicopter to the shotgun guard he has brought along to shoot down Sun, the last of the eagles. "We are Sun and men, too," says the leader of the rescuers.

"When the eagle is no more," the Medicine Man said, "then we are no more." Rancher Osmun says, "When something is finished, it's finished, forget it. We got a new evolution, the machine, this copter, a new bird." This is the serious issue, the conflict underneath the comic banter of the Navajos and underneath the romantic picture of the attractive young woman with her 30-30 rifle and horse. It is a conflict of values, a conflict of ideals.

Since before recorded history, the Navajo have believed in nature. The purpose of life, in their philosophy, is to live in a respectful relationship with the sun, the earth, and all things. To be, insofar as it is possible, part of sun and earth. To kill an eagle would be to kill part of the self. It would cut off the part of the self that communicates with the sun and the air.

Since the sixteenth century, probably, and certainly since the Industrial Revolution of the early 1800s, Ira Osmun's culture has believed in capitalism. The purpose of life, in capitalism's philosophy, is to invest capital and make profit. Everything else—respect for life, loyalty, honesty—is secondary. In the story, sheep are the capital investment. It is so large an investment that a helicopter is needed for "management"; the profit margin is so fragile that any threat to it must be eliminated ("controlled," in Osmun's vocabulary). This includes eagles, Navajos, and volunteer teachers.

The gun battle throws light on these values. The capitalist saves himself by giving his shotgun guard an early retirement option. The Indians do not save Sun, but they do help him by acting as targets to draw the enemy's machine-gun fire. When the action is all over and the guns are silenced, the reader wonders if Osmun's "new evolution," his "new bird," will dominate the world after all. As we learned from all those B-westerns, it is the good guys who ultimately win.

Will Bryant

b. 1923?

In Will Bryant's 1961 book *Great American Guns*, each story is inspired by a real incident involving a particular weapon. When it came time to write about the "Peacemaker" Colt, Bryant had a story close at hand. The eyewitness who tells this story is Will's own grandfather, Mince Bryant, who has always inspired him. "Gramp's voice," Bryant said in a recent letter to me, "is in all my books."

Bryant grew up on the move, attending as many as forty schools in places like Sheridan, Wyoming; Salt Lake City, Utah; Yuma, Arizona; and Portland, Oregon. During World War II he was a navy pilot, and after that he went to New York and worked as an illustrator, wood engraver, and designer. After writing *Great American Guns*, which he also illustrated, Bryant turned to writing fiction.

His novels include *The Big Lonesome* (1971), *Escape from Sonora* (1973), *Blue Russell* (1976), and *A Time for Heroes* (1987); he's now putting together another one, the working title of which is "The Wild Cards."

The Fastest Gun

You hear a heap of talk about fast guns these days. A fast gun in action was something to see, all right. I seen a few, here and there—I b'lieve the fastest was over in Indian Territory.

I remember it was the dustiest town I was ever in. Last thing before I went to catch the train, I took a bath at the barber shop. It was old hog-grease soap and it left more smell than it took out, but it settled the dust.

No, I wasn't a deputy any more when this happened. That was a line of work that never set too well with me. A man who wears a big hog-leg on his hip ought to be ready to use it and I never was. Oh, when I first went down into that country, I wanted to be *notorious*. I wore a pair of boots with stars on the front and heels so high it was like walkin' downhill. Then I went to work with the Indian Police in the Osage Nation and packed a big forty-four. There wasn't any other white allowed on the reservation. My job was to watch out for small-pox and help round up the horse thieves and outlaws who hid out in there. It was ticklish work.

For a while I had charge of the holdover, the jail where we kept those boys until the U.S. Marshal's deputies came for them. I had a cot to sleep on there in the office in front of the cells, and I used to lay there at night and listen to the stories. Once there was Wiley Haines and the one they called Bosco the Snake-Eater, both jugged at the same time. The yarns they told would curl your hair. They never did hold it against me that I carried the keys, but they had a way of lookin' sideways and a-watchin' me that let me know you wouldn't have to skin very deep to run into bear.

In those days, the Bill Doolin gang was broke up and Bill Doolin and Red Buck was both dead, along with Bitter Creek Newcomb. But there was still plenty of ornery customers around. When I quit the Indian Police, I went over to Ponca City. My brother, Bill, was a deputy there. One night I run into one of the outlaws I had kept locked up in the holdover. When he seen me, he looked disagreeable as a skinned snake in hot sand. I said I wasn't wearin' a badge anymore; so we went over to the hotel and had supper together and then set up half the night yarning.

He told me, "Kid, I had a bellyfull of this outlawin' around. It's got so they make too much trouble anymore, especially if you shoot a man." He said he had a piece of farmland—he didn't say where—and he aimed to work it. That was the last I seen of him. A day or two later, I told Brother Bill about it and he said, "Dadburn it, kid, why didn't you tell me?" I could see he was upset, but all I said was, "I ain't paid to catch your men."

Brother Bill wasn't like me—he was a real lawman. You could tell. He looked lop-sided without his gun and he had a bullet-notched ear. He had a way of coming into a room and closing the door with his foot, like he didn't want his hands full of doorknob at the wrong time. And he would stand there and size everybody up. There was some good marshals there in those days, like Heck Thomas and Bud Ledbetter and Bill Tilghman. Brother Bill was cut from the same hide.

They was all good with a gun. Fast? Well, fast enough. You didn't hear much about a man being *fast* with a gun. Folks would say that so-and-so was *good* with a gun. There's a difference. Being fast was a part of it, all right. But being *slow* was something, too.

No, I ain't forgot the story I was about to tell . . . Well, sir, after I put that badge away and sold the forty-four that went with it—I remember I got eleven dollars for it—I went back to the tailor's trade. I had been apprenticed to a tailor back home in Missouri. So I was what we called a boomer tailor. I would travel from town to town with a suitcase full of samples—suits and pants and a lot of bolt ends of woolen goods. Wherever I'd light, I'd set up shop right there. Barber shops was good because there was men in and out of there all day. Saloons had the traffic, too, but there the men wasn't interested in how their pants looked. When a man is getting all slicked up is the time he's most apt to think his pants is shabby. Right there while a man was getting a haircut or some curl and dye-color put to his mustache, I would make my pitch and show the goods I carried. When I made a sale I could take the feller's measurements and start cutting in the hotel room, or if there wasn't any hurry I would make up the britches later and deliver them next trip or mail them.

It's a funny thing . . . there wasn't much call for coats. Those men all spent a lot of time in the saddle. Pants went fast, but a coat would last forever. But times was hard then and there was precious little work—you know, a man would let his pants go till it was a scandal.

Where was I? That's right, I carried my suitcase over to the station to wait for the train. It was hot as a blister; I remember how the dust puffed underfoot with every step. There wasn't a soul on the street that time of day. The town was laid out on one side of the tracks. It wasn't much, only a few false-front buildings with a boardwalk. The train depot was only a tin roof set on some rough-sawed, four-by-four posts. The street lay between it and the buildings; all around was open country, rolling yellow prairie.

There was a big freight wagon standing across the street from the train shed and a team of dray horses switching clouds of flies off one another with their tails. Dogs sprawled here and there, asleep and twitching with dreams, or scratching. It was Indian Territory, remember, and for every Indian there was between three and seven dogs, at a guess. The way they used to bark and carry on at night would put your hackles up. . . . All right, I'll get on with it.

I walked into the shade under that tin roof and put down my suitcase, and set on it. There was only a little time till the train was due. Then I seen two men walking toward the depot shed where I was waiting. They had their heads together, talking as they walked, and one looked back over his shoulder now and then. They both wore suits and ties and shoes, not boots, and one wore a hard hat. But they walked like they was more used to straddling horses than footing it.

They walked right on by me and took a look down the track and then stood there in the shade a few feet away, still talking, their voices low, but excited—strained, maybe. The tall one took off his hat to mop his head and his coat pulled aside so I seen his Colt tucked in next to his ribs in a holster. Then I recognized him. I had seen him once over around Pawhuska where he was suspicioned of being in on a train robbery. That was all I knowed about him. The one in the hard hat was a stranger to me.

Well, sir, I was uneasy. I set there and wondered how it would look if I didn't catch the train. There wasn't a sound except the low hum of them two voices, or a little creak and jingle of harness when one of the horses would move under his canopy of flies. Sound just didn't carry in that heat. I almost didn't hear a slow clop-clop-clop from over beyond the line of buildings. You understand, now, none of this is what a feller generally remembers or pays any mind to—it's only because of what was a-goin' to happen that I remembered later, and let me tell you, it's still as clear as if it happened day before yesterday.

The sound of that wore-out horse had stopped. A minute later a man walked out the front door of the livery stable down the street. He wore boots and was all one color from the dust. There was a gun on his hip, but that wasn't uncommon. He walked along the boardwalk and started to go in the Chinaman's restaurant, when he seen me and them other two. He stopped half in the door; then he turned back toward us and stepped down into the street, a little more than fifty yards away and off to one side of the freight wagon. For the first time, I seen a little flash on his shirt front where his deputy's badge caught the sun.

I turned. The tall one stood there, froze, and his jaw hung down. Then his teeth come together with a snap like a beaver trap and his hand clawed past his coat for that gun. His partner, white as flour paste, grabbed ahold of his gun arm.

"No, don't do it!" he screeched, but the tall one grunted and throwed him off and that gun came out. *Fast!*

That was when the lid blowed off. I was right in the way and caught the muzzle blast from that first shot. Little sparks of burnt powder stung my cheek and neck, and my ears clanged like a skillet you've beat on a rock. I jumped like a scorched cat and scampered behind one of the posts—it wasn't far away and it wasn't safe, but it was all there was. The dray horses come alive and bucked in the harness and dogs was running all ways and yelping.

The deputy had stopped and pulled his gun—he was about as fast as a man reaching for his watch to see if it's time for lunch. The outlaw—*he* was fast. That big Colt roared and bucked and each time a long streamer of smoke would lance out. The deputy squared away, both feet planted, and he settled his gun butt into the upturned palm of his left hand, a two-handed grip, both hands right straight out in front of him. Then he fired.

There was a puff of dust and padding flew out the back of the outlaw's coat—*fffss-s-t!*—like that. The threads sailed back in a long arc and floated down. His gun bucked once more, and at the same time the deputy fired again . . . and again . . . like that, timed slow; and each time there was a little puff of dust like the first one. On the third shot, the outlaw come uncoupled and slid out from under his hat.

There wasn't a sound. Black powder smoke hung in the air under that shed roof so thick you could swing on it. When the shooting stopped, the dogs all stopped running—they were everyplace, tails tucked and all hunkered down and shivering. The outlaw's partner had run off a ways with his hands in the air. The deputy hadn't moved a muscle. That Colt was still right out there in front of him and the hammer was eared back. There was a big wheezing sigh; one of the dray horses buckled and dropped to its knees, then flopped over against the wagon tongue. It was shot through the heart.

Somewhere a door slammed. I come out from behind the post. The deputy still hadn't moved—you wouldn't call him rash. A dark patch showed on his right leg, just above the knee. I walked toward him then, out from under the tin roof and into the sunlight and I seen his eyes glare at me over that gun barrel.

"You're hurt," I said. "Can I give you a hand?"

"Hurt . . ." he said. "Hurt? Why that so-and-so couldn't hurt me." He looked burned up that I had thought it.

"I reckon not," I said. I could see the blood running into his boot.

Then he finally eased his gun down. He walked over to where the outlaw lay and bent down and picked the man's Colt out of the dust. He punched out the empties; every shot had been fired.

A crowd began to gather and mill around. The dogs went to scratching again. The freighter had found his dead horse and was hollering who was going to pay for it. The deputy looked right through him and limped off. A meat-cutter with a dirty apron and his own cloud of flies asked me did I see the shooting. I said yes and he said that deputy must've been fast.

"No," I said, "it was the other one who was fast."

A little later, the train finally come in and I climbed aboard. That night when I got off the train in El Reno and got to a hotel, I opened up my suitcase and there in the folds of woolen pants goods was a forty-four bullet. It was hardly mashed. Must've been that first shot, I thought, the one that stung me. I went to sleep with my ears still buzzing and I was thinking how fast that outlaw was with a gun and what it had got him.

He was fast, all right.

Quick Justice in the Old West

"Disagreeable as a skinned snake in hot sand." "I jumped like a scorched cat." These homespun similes can be found sprinkled all through this yarn by Will Bryant. He is also good at creating low-key understatements: "It was ticklish work," he says of rounding up horse thieves and outlaws deep in Indian Territory. After an outlaw fires six shots into the general vicinity of a deputy, "the deputy still hadn't moved—you wouldn't call him rash."

Bryant's writing style lends "The Fastest Gun" an authentic tone, but even more authenticity can be discovered in his historical allusions.

For instance, the story can be accurately dated by its numerous references to actual people and places. The "Osage Nation" refers to a time between 1872, when the Osage Indians were settled in the Oklahoma territory, and 1907, when Oklahoma became a state. President Harrison opened the "Indian Territory" for white settlement in 1889. The "kid," therefore, is in the territory somewhere around that date.

But we can nail it down tighter than that. "In those days, the Bill Doolin gang was broke up. . . . Bill Doolin and Red Buck was both dead, along with Bitter Creek Newcomb." Bill Doolin, who started his career with the Daltons (but didn't end up getting killed with them in Coffeyville, Kansas), gained outlaw notoriety in about 1892. In 1896 he was captured by deputy marshal Bill Tilghman but escaped. In August of 1896, deputy marshal Heck Thomas cornered Doolin and invited him to surrender. Doolin replied with a rifle but missed, and Heck Thomas ended the conversation with a blast from his shotgun. He did not miss.

Rufus "Red" Buck, along with his four fellow desperadoes, was executed by hanging in 1896. They were sentenced by the "Hanging Judge," Isaac Charles Parker, who ordered the hanging of 160 men during his bench career in Indian Territory. Thomas, Tilghman, and Bud Ledbetter, all mentioned in Bryant's story, worked as U.S. deputy marshals for Judge Parker during the 1890s.

As for Bitter Creek Newcomb, he and his sidekick Charlie Pierce were separated from the Doolin gang after a train robbery in May of 1895 and decided to hole up in a farmhouse near Guthrie, Oklahoma. Like Doolin, Pierce and Newcomb elected to shoot it out with U.S. deputy marshals. When the smoke cleared, the outlaws had been thoroughly perforated and each one had enough lead in him to start a bullet factory.

Bryant's references to guns are authentic, too. The "Peacemaker" Colt, as it was called, was introduced in 1873. Although it was a centerfire cartridge revolver, it still used black powder and produced the kind of smoke that Bryant describes. From all accounts, a Peacemaker in the hands of a calm and competent marksman would live up to its nickname.

Gerald Haslam

b. 1937

Gerald Haslam is a lifelong resident of the mythical frontier's far western edge—the coastal region of northern California. In his youth he worked as an oil field roustabout, picked crops, packed vegetables and fruits, and was employed as a clerk. He is now a professor of English at Sonoma State College.

Haslam bases his fictional characters on ordinary people of the working classes, mostly those of the Great Central Valley of California. His stories create a kind of mosaic, illustrating a culture that takes its living from thriving oil fields as well as rich farmland. *Twentieth Century Western Writers* quotes him as saying, "I write about a California that is still western—that 70% of the state that remains small town or rural: ranches, farms, vast wilderness tracts . . . hard working people of all colors, who struggle to survive on a harsh landscape."

More often than not, Haslam's stories center around a strong sense of place and an equally strong awareness of cultural diversity. The combination often leads his characters into conflicts that are as raw as they are turbulent.

Among his short story collections are *That Constant Coyote*, *California Stories*, *The Man Who Cultivated Fire, and Other Stories*, *Snapshots: Glimpses of the Other California*, *Okies*, and *The Wages of Sin*.

Cowboys

This old boy named Shorty Moore used to haul mud out to the rig, see. Shorty he could whup a man and he never ducked a fight, so not many guys in the oilfields ever give him much trouble.

One time old Shorty he was sitting around the doghouse at quitting time while us guys changed to go home, and this engineer looked at Shorty's duds, then asked Shorty real smart alecky if he was a cowboy. All of us on the crew just set back to watch Shorty stomp the bastard, see, but old Shorty he fooled us. He looked around, kind of grinned, and said real quiet: Naw, I ain't no cowboy. Never have been. But I wear these boots and this belt and shirt because they're western, see, working men's clothes. And I feel western. I ain't no college sissy with a necktie and pink hands. I'm a man and that's what my clothes say. Any old boy that doubts it ain't got but to jump and I'll kick his ass for him.

That was that. The engineer never said nothing more, so old Shorty just let things slide and I guess everyone was happy to get out of the doghouse that afternoon.

But, you know, everytime a guy turns around in Bakersfield some pasty-faced bastard's eyeing your belt buckle or boots, and you just know he's a-thinking *cowboy* and laughing at you to hisself. They all think they're high powers. I ain't like old Shorty; things like that just eat on me. I work as hard as any man does for my wages, a-bucking pig iron on a drilling rig, and I can't take some pencil-necked fairy that works in a office looking down his nose at me. I'll break his nose for him, by God.

Last summer whenever the college kids come out to replace guys going on vacation, wouldn't you know we'd get us a hippy. And it was comical as hell when this kid first drove up to the rig. We'd just spudded in, see, a-hoping to hit gas on Suisun Bay up near Fairfield. It was tower change and my crew was working daylights. About the time we walked out of the doghouse, and old Turk Brown's crew was coming off, see, up sputters this little red sports car with a great big long-haired kid a-driving it. Well, he gets out of the car, all the guys just kind of standing back watching him, and he commences talking to the pusher. That kid was so huge, and his car was so small, he looked like a big old snake coming out of a little basket: more and more of him kept coming after you just knew the car couldn't hold no more.

Old Arkie Williams he made a kissing sound with his mouth and the kid looked at him. I seen cold eyes before, but that kid looked like he could put a fire out staring at it. And I could see that even though Arkie kept on bullshitting, he knew he made a mistake. Is it a boy or a girl? Arkie said. He never did have enough sense to admit he was wrong after he started spouting off. The pusher told us to get up on the rig and pull them slips, and the kid was still just a-looking at Arkie, not saying nothing; I figured Arkie was into it. Too bad for him too. He never could fight a lick.

The kid went to work that morning and spent the whole tower helping Buford Kileen clean out the pumps. Come quitting time, we all headed for the doghouse hot to get changed and go drink us some beer. Just about the time Arkie walked up to the doorway from between pipe racks, the new kid stepped in front of him and bam! one punch cold cocked him. Jesus, could that big old kid punch! And that ain't all; Arkie hadn't but hit the ground and the kid had him kicked three or four times. We grabbed the kid and had one hell of a time holding him while two boys from the crew that was just coming to work helped Arkie. The pusher took the kid into his office and told him, I guess, any more fighting and he'd be canned. And the pusher took Arkie aside and told him he'd got just what he deserved.

What really got me though was that the new kid never said nothing. After it was over he just got out of his work clothes and climbed into suede drawers with fringes on 'em, and high cowboy boots, and a western belt with a big turquois buckle. He put on some little colored beads and a leather sombrero and out he walked, no shirt at all. He climbed into his little red car, see, and drove off without saying goodbye or kiss my ass or nothing.

After he was gone some of the guys commenced kidding about the high falutin cowboy clothes the kid wore. I'll bet he never rode nothing but that little red car, old Buford said, cept maybe a few of them college coeds. Everyone laughed. Yeah, Easy Ed Davis said, he's a real cowpoke that one, must think he's Buffalo Bill with that long hair. Reckon we ought to buy him some ribbons to go with them beads? I asked. Arkie never laughed, then pretty soon he ups and says that if the kid ever messed with him again, by God, there'd be one more cowboy on Boot Hill. Shorty Moore showed up a little later at this beer joint where we usually went, and he said he didn't have no use for hippies period. No use a-tall.

The kid turned out to be one hell of a worker; he give a honest jump for his wages, I'll say that much. He never let none of the boys on the job get real friendly with him, but he seemed to like it when they commenced calling him Cowboy. He didn't know that most of the guys wanted to call him Dude, but they thought better of it. He was a big old boy.

I could tell he really didn't give a damn for none of us. Whenever he did talk to us it was to show off all of his book learning and to hint at how ignorant he figured we was. You know, one of us might say he thought the Dodgers would go all the way this year, and young Cowboy would kind of sneer: It all depends on whether they can exploit more blacks than the other teams, he'd say, shit like that. Hell, he couldn't stand to see us enjoy nothing; he liked to wreck things for everyone it seemed like. Cowboy was studying to be a college pro-fessor and he had about that much sense.

A couple of months after he first come to work, we finally lifted the kid. He was tougher than most summer hires to trick because he didn't talk much, and he didn't seem to give a damn about what we thought of him. But old Easy Ed, our derrick man, he finally bullshitted the kid into it. Easy Ed could talk a nigger white if you give him half a chance. He just kept a-grabbing at Cowboy all the time, see, telling him he didn't know what a strong man was. Hell, old Ed would say, a young buck like you ain't seen a stout man till you seen a old timer like me hot after it. There ain't many old boys in this oil patch can lift as much weight as me, by God. I can pick up three guys at one time. Easy Ed's just a little bitty fart, and the kid would kind of look at him funny but not say nothing. It was comical, really. Cowboy would bring all these books with him to read when he ate, but he'd no more than get his dinner bucket open than Easy Ed would be a-chewing on his ear. I believe that kid finally give in just to shut Ed up.

We was circulating mud and waiting for the engineers to give us the go ahead on making more hole that day; everyone was pretty bored. We'd just finished unloading sacks of chemicals off Shorty's truck, and we was kind of laying around on the mud rack chewing tobacco and telling lies. Pretty soon up comes Easy Ed and he right away starts in on Cowboy. Before long the kid said O.K., let's see you lift three guys.

So everybody trooped around behind the rig, and old Ed laid down a length of rope on the ground. Then he said: three of you boys lay down on her. Heavy, he said to me, you take one side. Shorty you take the other. Cowboy, you crawl in the middle. I want you to know there ain't no trick to it. We three got down on our backs while the other guys stood around us. Ed just kept a-jabbering, see. I swear, that guy should of been a preacher; he damn sure could of talked some sisters into the bushes.

Well, anyways, old Ed tells us three to wrap our arms and legs around each other (me and Shorty knowing this stuff from way back, but not letting on, so the kid won't suspect nothing). Now make her real tight, Ed tells us, I don't want anybody slipping when I pick y'all up. Me and Shorty really cinched up on the kid's arms and legs, see. We had him pinned to the ground and I could tell he was catching on.

Ed, a-yacking all the time, commenced unbuttoning Cowboy's fly and Buford handed Ed the dope brush. The kid tensed up, then kind of chuckled and relaxed. Ah shit, he said, laughing a little, I figured then it was gonna be a easy lifting, and that the kid wasn't half bad after all. But just about the time Easy Ed starting painting the kid's balls with dope, old Arkie couldn't keep his mouth shut. He kind of spit at the kid: In the position you let us get you in, weavil, just thank of all the thangs we *could* do to you. Then he made that kissing sound.

Oh Jesus! The kid just exploded! I'm a pretty stout old boy myownself, see, but Cowboy just sort of shook me loose, then kicked Ed in the slats with his free foot. I've helped lift maybe a hundred weavils in my day, and nobody never just shook me off before. Old Shorty hung on and in a minute the two of them was rolling around in the dust and puncture vines. Shorty don't know how to give up in a fight, and he held on to that big old boy like a dog on a bull.

We knew the pusher would can the kid if he seen him fighting, so we all jumped in and broke her up. When we managed to get them apart, the kid's eyes locked on Shorty, and Shorty he stuck his finger in the kid's face and said: Name the place Cowboy. We'll finish her where there ain't nobody gonna get in the way. The kid just kept staring and said anyplace was fine with him.

There was this little beer joint at a eucalyptus grove between where we was drilling and Rio Vista. That's where Shorty and the kid decided to meet after work. The whole crew drove right over there and drank beer while they waited for Shorty to get back from Lodi where he left his truck in the chemical company's yard every evening. The kid he stayed outside a-leaning on his little red car, see, his sombrero tilted back, his long hair a-blowing in the wind. Them frozen blue eyes of his just glowed. Damned if he don't look like some oldtime gunfighter, Buford said looking out the window. I told him that was one cowboy I didn't want to tangle with. You notice he never messes with me no more, Arkie bragged, and all the guys laughed, but old Arkie was serious and he didn't see nothing funny. Naturally, Easy Ed took to laying bets: I taken old Shorty, he said, and I'll put five bucks on him. Buford covered him right away. Arkie bet on Shorty too, and Buford covered him. Ain't you a-betting Heavy? Ed asked me, but I said no. I didn't feel too good about the whole thing.

Shorty drove up directly and crawled out of his Chevy. For a minute him and Cowboy just stood there staring at each other, then Cowboy he bent over and reached into his car and pulled out a gunbelt, the old kind with ammunition loops and long thongs dangling from the holster. He slipped her on and tied the thongs around his right thigh. Hey! I heard Buford say and when I looked away from the kid, I seen old Shorty was doing the same thing.

All of us guys froze where we was. Cowboy and Shorty they pulled their six-guns from the holsters, spun the cylinders and kinda blew on the sights. Then they slid the revolvers back into leather and commenced walking toward one another. What the hell is this? Easy Ed whispered, but I couldn't answer, my heart was a-stompin inside my chest and I couldn't even swallow. I wanted to holler, but I just stood there.

When they was about twenty-five or thirty feet apart—real close—Cowboy and Shorty stopped, then spread their legs like they was gonna pick up something heavy. It's yer play, dude, Shorty said, his eyes pointed straight at Cowboy's. Cowboy he kinda rocked back on his heels: You've been alive too long, he croaked. You've out-lived yourself.

Then the roar! In what seemed like a forever of sound, they dipped their right shoulders and threw their right hands straight down. There wasn't no fancy grabbing and winging, movie-style, just two short, efficient moves, like when a good worker shovels.

And Shorty busted backwards, almost up in the air, then fell in a heap, a puppet without strings, empty, his gun in the dirt. A cloud of blue smoke hung where he'd stood.

Oh sweet lovin Jesus! I cried out, and I run over to Shorty, but he'd had it. He was all sprawled out, his eyes looking like egg-whites. Little frothy bubbles was coming from his brisket, but not much blood. He coughed, choked maybe, and a gusher shot up from his mouth and from the hole in his middle, then the bubbles quit.

Get your ass away from him, I heard Cowboy say. I looked at the kid. He still held his six-gun, and the blue smoke still hung there in front of him; there wasn't no wind. I looked back down at Shorty and seen a great big puddle of blood was growing underneath him, peeking out, not red but kinda maroon, almost black. Get! Cowboy hollered again, so I walked back to where the other boys stood. I couldn't do old Shorty no good.

Cowboy holstered his pistol, untied the thong, then slipped the gunbelt off and dropped it into his car. You guys gonna buy me a beer? he asked. None of us said nothing. I didn't figure so, he said. He climbed into his car, backed up—me afraid he was agonna run over Shorty but he was real careful not to—then started out onto the road. Then he done something real funny; he slowed down, almost stopped, and flashed us one of them V-peace signs hippies are always making. He drove away toward Fairfield, up over a low hill into the fading sun.

Jesus, Buford said, what're we gonna do?

Easy Ed he just kept looking from where Shorty lay with a big old blow-fly already doing business on his bloody lower lip, then back toward the hill where Cowboy'd disappeared. We might could form a posse, he said.

The Old Code of the New West

"'You've been alive too long,' he croaked. 'You've outlived yourself.'"

It is a familiar tale: some guy has a reputation for being tough, but then along comes a younger guy who is tougher and quicker. The younger guy gets older and slower, and another one comes along to take his place. It happens over and over, and shows up in story after story.

Throughout the short and violent history of America's western frontier there has always been some new breed of fighter, someone to replace the out-of-date protagonist. The best example is probably Jack Schaefer's character Shane, whose six-gun puts an end to Fletcher, one of the last of the open-range oligarchs, as well as Fletcher's gunman, Wilson.

"Naw, I ain't no cowboy," Shorty Moore admits. But in spite of what he says, he owns a gunfighter rig that looks like it came from the old West. Shorty also believes in a certain code of behavior, a belief that forces him to demand some respect. Nostalgia for a violent era and pride are Shorty's two fatal flaws. What he has forgotten—what all the roughnecks on the oil rig have forgotten—is that in the old West there was always a faster gun, always another man who demanded respect.

Haslam's shootout between the old fighter and the young one has a timeless quality to it. It is a new story, yet it seems familiar. The story is based on the familiar plot in which a "greenhorn" or newcomer is sneered at, then ridiculed, before finally being initiated by the older men. In most stories the newcomer takes his hazing with good humor and then somehow turns the tables on his new friends and gets even with them.

Haslam's ending is a surprise: most male dominance rituals do not result in death. Like rutting elk or battling bighorns, men may shove each other around and make a lot of noise, but the aim of it is to drive off the other male, not to kill him.

"Cowboy," the hippy, resembles Shane, or the Lone Ranger. He comes to town as a quiet stranger who doesn't want trouble but soon encounters evil or injustice. He waits for the bad guys to make their move, then vanquishes them (often just by killing or capturing their leader). Then he rides off, usually into the sunset: this symbolizes the fact that his day, too, will soon end. The only thing different in Haslam's story is that Cowboy rides off in a red sports car.

Haslam's mob of roughnecks is interesting. Individually they are competent, tough, and good-humored. They tend to talk big, but their buddies never "call them out" to prove their boasts. They work hard all day, like cowpunchers, then go to the saloon together. They are a strong group. But when they lose their leader, they don't know what to do.

The roughnecks realize, dimly, that they have just witnessed an age-old ritual. They remember how the story is supposed to end: "We might could form a posse," Ed says. But they won't, because it wouldn't do Shorty any good. And, like Shorty, Cowboy will someday outlive himself, too.

Bill Pronzini

b. 1943

Bill Pronzini, one of the West's most prolific writers and editors, has more than fifty novels and some three hundred stories, reviews, articles, and essays to his credit. His pen names include Jack Foxx, William Jeffrey, Alex Saxon, and Romer Zane Grey.

Pronzini has edited and coedited more than eighty collections of western, detective, and science fiction stories. He is also a devoted fan of the old-time pulps; according to David Whitehead in *Twentieth Century Western Writers*, Pronzini's "knowledge of the genre and its writers is now almost encyclopedic."

Pronzini's latest is a novel titled *Demons* (1993), which features his popular "Nameless Detective"—a character who appears in twenty-two of his mystery books. Also among his recent publications are two western novels, *The Hangings* and *Firewind*. In collaboration with Martin H. Greenberg, he has been responsible for a series of "Best of the West" classic western stories. This series includes stories of lawmen, outlaws, and cowboys; it recently began to include stories based on regional themes.

Righteous Guns

It was hot.

And quiet—too quiet.

He walked slowly along the dusty street, one hand resting on the Colt Peacemaker pouched at his hip. The harsh midday sun made the false-fronted buildings stand out in sharp relief against a sky more white than blue, like an alkali flat turned upside down. Heat mirage shimmered beyond the livery stable in the next block, half obscuring the road that led up into the foothills west of town.

He paused opposite the Lucky Lady Saloon and Gambling Hall and stood hip-shot, listening to the silence. Nothing moved anywhere ahead of him or around him. There were no horses tied to the hitchrails, no wagons or buckboards, no townspeople making their way along the plank sidewalks. But he could feel eyes watching him from behind closed doors and shuttered windows.

Waiting, all of them—just as he was.

Waiting for the lawmen and their righteous guns.

Sweat worked its way out from under his Stetson; he wiped it away with the back of his left hand, smearing the dust-cake on his lean, sun-weathered face. His mouth tasted dry and dusty, like the street itself, and he thought of pushing in through the saloon's batwings for a beer and a shot of rye. But liquor dulled a man's thoughts, turned his reflexes slow. No liquor today.

From his shirt pocket he took out the makings and rolled a cigarette with his left hand. He scratched a sulfur match into flame on the sole of his boot. His right hand didn't move from the butt of his Peacemaker in its hand-tooled Mexican holster.

How many of them would there be? Close to a dozen, likely, maybe more. Robbing the Cattlemen's and Merchant's Bank as he'd done this morning, shooting down the bank director, Leo Furman, in cold blood when he wouldn't open the safe . . . those were about as serious crimes as there were in the Territory. There'd be plenty in the posse, all right. They'd want him bad, them and their righteous guns.

Not that it mattered much, he thought. A wry smile bent the corners of his mouth. He'd faced lawmen before, in numbers from one to twenty, in towns like this one in half a dozen states and territories throughout the West. This was nothing new. This was just more of the same for a man like him.

It was only a question of time. He'd wait, because there was nothing else for him to do. He hadn't got the money from the bank; Leo Furman had tried for a hideout gun and he'd had to shoot him before Furman could open the safe. So the only thing he could do was wait. Better to face them here, than run and have them chase him down like a dog.

When they came, he'd be ready for them.

He blew smoke into the hot still air and then commenced walking again, thinking about Leo Furman. A bossy, fussy man; like so many bank directors, he'd thought that the money other men entrusted to him gave him power over those men. Demanding, high and mighty, full of contempt— that was Furman. He wasn't sorry he'd killed the bastard. He wasn't sorry at all.

He moved on past Benson's Mercantile, the Elite Cafe, the Palace Hotel. There was still no sound, nothing stirring in the thick, milky heat. It was as if the town itself was holding its breath now.

On past the Eternal Rest Funeral Home, the blacksmith's shop, the deserted sheriff's office; heading toward the hostler's. He knew just what a menacing figure he cut, moving along that dusty, barren street: big, hard face full of angles and shadows, body leaned down to sinew and bone. Most men stood aside when he passed, avoiding his eyes. So did the women. They were afraid of him, the women; the only way he'd ever had one was by money or by force.

Sometimes, late at night, he would wake up in a strange bed or by the remains of a trailside fire and think of what might have been. An end to the vicious swath he cut through the West; an end to the shooting and the killing of decent men; righteous guns instead of his own desperate ones, or better yet, no guns at all. The love of a good woman, a small ranch on good grazing land . . .

Something moved in the alley between the blacksmith's shop and the livery.

A shadow, then a second shadow.

He tensed, alert to the sudden smell of danger. He slowed to a walk, pitched his cigarette away, let his fingers curl loosely around the butt of his Peacemaker. Squinted through the hard glare of the sunlight.

More movement inside the alley. Over on the far side of the street, too, behind Baldwin's Feed and Grain Store. Furtive sounds reached his ears: the soft sliding of boots in the dust, the faint thump of an arm or hand or leg against wood.

They were here.

Most times they came openly, riding in on their horses, weapons at the ready. Once in a while, though, they came in quiet and slinking like this, to wait in ambush in the shadows. No better than he was, then. In their own way, just as desperate.

Well, it didn't matter.

It was time, and as always, he was ready.

"*Hold it right there, Gaines!*" a voice roared suddenly from the alley. "*We've got you surrounded!*"

He bent his knees and let himself bow slightly at the middle. But he was scowling now. Gaines, the voice had said. How did they know his real name?

"*You can't get away, Gaines! Stand where you are and raise your hands over your head!*"

There was something about that voice, the odd thunderous tone of it, as if it were coming through a megaphone, that made him feel suddenly uneasy. More than uneasy—strange, dizzy. His head began to ache. The sun-baked street, the false-fronted buildings, seemed to shift in and out of focus, to take on new and different dimensions. Sunstroke, he thought. I been standing out here in the heat too long.

But it wasn't sunstroke . . .

One of the shadows in the alley shifted into view—his first clear glimpse of the law. And he stared, for the lawdog wasn't wearing Levi's or broad-brimmed hat or tin star pinned to vest or cotton shirt; wasn't carrying Winchester rifle or Colt sixgun. Strange blue uniform, blue helmet, weapon in one hand like none he'd ever seen before.

He stood blinking, confused. And saw then that the buildings didn't just have false fronts; they had false backs too, and no backs at all on some of them, just a latticework of wooden supports like sets in a play.

Sets in a *movie.*

Movie sets, TV-show sets on the back lot of Mammoth Pictures.

A dozen movies, a hundred TV shows, all starring Roy Gaines in the role of the villain . . . and Leo Furman, the director, always telling him what to do, treating him with contempt, never once letting him be good and decent, never once letting him be the hero . . . wouldn't open his safe, wouldn't give him the money he needed to pay his gambling debts, and so he'd shot Furman dead, just as he would any damned fool who crossed him . . . and then he'd come here, because there was no place else for him to go, a man on the run, killer on the run, here to make still another last stand . . .

"Gaines! You can't escape! Raise your hands over your head! Don't make us do this the hard way!"

The hard way, the hard way, the hard way . . .

There was a jolting in his mind; the false-fronted buildings, the sun-blasted street settled back into familiar focus. Then, ahead, he could see four, five, six of the possemen fanning out toward him, keeping to cover. A grim smile formed on his mouth. He'd done all this before, so many times before. He knew just what to do. He didn't even have to think about it.

"All right," he yelled, "come and get it, boys!" His hand went down, came up again with his desperate gun blazing—

And the righteous guns cut him down.

False Fronts and Real Lead

Careful readers, the kind who notice each little component of a story, will appreciate the subtle details that Bill Pronzini uses to build up the suspense in "Righteous Guns." Who is this man with the Colt Peacemaker? Where is this town? And why are the "righteous guns" waiting for him?

Look closer. Everything seems to be a cliché, from the Peacemaker and the Stetson to the name of the Lucky Lady Saloon, the false fronts, and the plank sidewalk. It's too phony, too much like a cardboard cutout of a town. It is unpopulated—no horses, no wagons, no people. Yet the gunslinger feels the eyes watching him.

His long, lonely walk down the deserted street is a cliché. Even the suspense seems like something from a stock western movie. And the gunslinger's list of crimes, the ones he thinks about as he walks the long street—aren't there too many for one man?

Pronzini manipulates the tempo in this story, making the pace of the action match the gunman's steps, right to the center of the narrative. There it turns. Now the mysterious details really begin to build up. A lawman without a Winchester, in a blue uniform? A megaphone?

Then Gaines is hit by a sudden lapse into "reality," and in a brief lucid moment he recognizes both the actual situation and its inescapable ending. There's no modern moral to it, either, no judgment of the ways of the old West. It is just a plausible account of what might happen to a man who loses track of the line between fiction and actuality, between the legendary old West and the new, between who he is and who he has been told he is.

Mark Holden

b. 1951

"The Field" was originally published in *Southwest Review*. Other journals that have published stories by Mark Holden include *Mendocino*, *Sun Dog*, *Sonora*, and *High Plains*, indicating that the academic world takes Holden's creative writing seriously. But his interests reach beyond fiction. He has also had archery and bowhunting articles in *Upland Hunting*, *Bowhunter*, and *Outdoor Life*, and he was a finalist for the Massachusetts Arts Foundation Award in Playwriting. He holds an M.F.A. degree from the University of Massachusetts.

Holden's knowledge of animals and hunting and his ability to create multidimensional situations have more recently taken him into the area of graphic arts. His wildlife art and wood sculpture is now on exhibit in Lake Placid, New York, and Burlington, Vermont. He has been nominated for a supporting grant sponsored by the Andy Warhol Foundation, the National Endowment for the Arts, and the Rockefeller Foundation.

The Field

John Jenson was a small, wiry, and stubborn man who believed in God and lived in northern Vermont. He trapped for a living and hunted for food with a .308 Winchester. At fifty-four, despite arthritic flare-ups from rainy weather or tripping in a tangle of mountain laurel and bumping his knees, he still had the strength to carry a two-hundred-pound buck on his back through the woods.

Besides God, John believed in the practical efficiency of a fast bullet and a sharp knife. He reduced his needs to simplify his life and melted sleet, snow, and frozen dawns into a single element: weather. Although he could tell a sow bear from a boar at fifty yards, knowing their sex was unimportant. He believed meat was meat—something to fill his gut—so he aimed for the heart regardless.

John's way of thinking also allowed him to meet each day like every other; anything that interrupted the pattern of his routine was, he thought, an intervention of God. Last spring, his tarpapered lean-to filled with stacked wood was burned to the ground by lightning. Rather than rebuild it, he simply covered the wood with canvas. When God struck again in the form of a weasel to kill his chickens, John decided he did not need them; he could eat biscuits and coffee for breakfast instead of eggs.

After eating a rabbit which had snared itself in a wire loop dangling from a sapling, John drove his Jeep up to a clover field where the October sun had dropped so far below the horizon that only the blackest shades of blue remained. He drove on Tarbell Road past juniper pastureland and maple, oak, and birch woodlots with rockwalled boundaries, beyond Wells Road and the cornfields. At a particular spot where the blackberry hedges opened up from each other—stalks bent, broken, and wilting—he drove off the road. The tires pressed the clover flat in two sidewinding paths.

He scanned the field with headlights and a chrome spotlight bolted on the front fender of the driver's side until one beam settled on two small objects shining like oversized fireflies. Reflecting back the glowing whiteness of the lights, they remained fixed in the blinding glare; appeared suspended and alone in their dark surroundings, strangely separate from the animal's gray body.

The deer stood by itself in the open field bordered by hardwoods. The trees, with their limbs passing, touching, and intertwining, dry of sap but still heavy-leafed, built a natural wall of darkness around the field, and the starless sky, lit only by moon haze behind the drifting clouds, seemed brighter than it really was.

John Jenson squeezed the trigger of his rifle. He felt the butt of the walnut stock bury itself in his shoulder, heard the blast's echo fade in the trees. The deer ran forty yards with a hole through its heart before it dropped in the field near a barbed-wire fence.

John cut the fat doe open from ass to ribcage with a drop-point knife and separated the skin with an upward cutting motion to avoid slicing gut. He let the intestines spill out then cut through the diaphragm and, when he reached up into the chest cavity, felt the body heat rise and escape. His bloody fingers searched for the heart—more solid to the touch among the soft and spongy lungs; he looked for the liver in the gut pile. After wiping bits of clover and soil from the tender meat, he put it in a plastic bag and tucked it away inside his shirt.

John hung the carcass from an oak hidden back in the forest so it could cool in the night air. He used braided lengths of haybale twine tied together for a rope. The deer spun slowly one way, back again. Its hind feet hung high off the ground—a fox or bear could not reach up and tear the flanks. Smiling at the thought that God had not intervened, but allowed him to shoot this fine deer, John walked across the field to his Jeep and drove down a winding dirt road to his cabin.

Ed Philips was coming out the front door when John arrived. He wore a wide brimmed gray hat tilted to the left to offset his head, which dangled over his right shoulder because his left leg was longer than the other, and by tilting his head his natural limp was less pronounced, although his whole body looked as crooked as a wind-twisted branch on a scrub pine. He also wore green pants with a lighter, shinier green stripe running down each leg and smoked a stubby cigar which he constantly relit. This relighting was the reason his moustache never seemed to grow. Long, wispy gray hairs flourished at the corners of his lips, but the hairs beneath his nose were regularly singed and burnt back like unwanted brush.

Ed's face was very white and glassy smooth in the headlights' rays. A 30-.06 bolt-action Remington, with mounted scope and arm sling, balanced in his bony hands and rested crossways to his body.

John parked his Jeep beside the warden's newer truck. Two lights on the truck's roof flashed lazily and illuminated their faces in alternate bursts of red and blue.

"What are you doin' here?" John said.

"Hi, John. Cool out tonight." The warden removed the cigar from his lips and smiled with his tongue poking out between brown teeth.

"Yeah. What were you doin' inside?" John remembered, as if suddenly stepping barefooted on a thorn, that he had neglected to lock the door. Hardly anyone ventured this far on the dirt road that led to his cabin, but he usually locked the door to keep stray hunters from stealing furs or traps hung on the back wall. He had not locked the door this time because his dog, Nikoda, had chosen to remain inside, and the airedale, as wiry and stubborn as its master, would always defend the cabin from intruders.

Ed Philips shuffled his feet. He tilted his head forward to shield himself from the headlights' glare. "I was lookin' for you," he said. "Thought you'd be inside, listenin' to Mozart." He planted the cigar in the hole made vacant by his tongue.

"You got no right to enter when I ain't home."

"Door weren't locked. Thought you were inside, poppin' corn," Ed grinned.

John looked beyond Philips. The front door was half-open behind him. Where is my dog? he thought. Nikoda never let anyone in the cabin when he was left alone—especially someone like Ed Philips, with his head hung one way, his hip jutting out like a warped barnboard, and that longer leg dragging his foot in a black boot.

"You shoot my dog?"

"You've been shootin' deer out of season again. If I catch you, you're gonna have to pay a fine. Maybe go to jail."

"What? I ast you a question."

The warden ejected a shell from his rifle. The brass casing spun through the air and landed among pine needles. "He jumped me."

Knotted muscles raised the veins in John's forearms. "Get off my property."

"I'm here to warn you, Jenson. These are my woods, my responsibility. I don't want any deer shot out of season."

"These ain't your woods," John said.

"Where are you going?" Ed said.

"These ain't nobody's woods. But if they was they'd be mine, because I've lived in them for forty-nine years." He reached for his rifle on the front seat.

"Hold it!" Ed shouted. He aimed the scope's crosshairs at the back of John's head.

John turned. "You crippled son of a bitch dog-killer."

"Back off, Jenson. Don't try anything. Don't move a inch. Your mangy dog jumped me, so I shot him."

"Nikoda was inside."

"Sure he was! I went in lookin' for you, and he jumped me!"

"You had no right."

"No right? I'm the game warden!" Ed said. Then he added, "You oughtn't to leave your door unlocked if you don't want no visitors. Besides what you gettin' so worked up about? Damn dog was a menace. Crazy mean."

"Now, throw your gun over there." Ed nodded toward the pines.

"I ain't throwing my rifle."

"Put it there," Ed conceded. "Lay it down nice and slow." Ed climbed into his truck; the door slammed shut with a hollow clang to enclose the cab. He did not hang his rifle on the rack behind the seat but kept it pointed out the window as he drove away.

His brakelights flashed, bounced, and dipped over ruts and shallow gulleys before disappearing behind a wall of scrub oak and blueberries.

John grabbed his rifle and aimed through the trees. He fired once and sent a bullet through a branch. It deflected downward and ricochetted off a rock, made a strange whining sound. For a moment the clouds opened up, and the moonlight cast shadows, and silhouettes of wind-felled trees lay blackly on the forest floor.

It was cool all right, John thought. He could feel the air lose its warmth and autumn's chill creep in among the rustle of drying leaves.

Inside the cabin, where traps hung from wooden pegs tapped into drilled holes, Nikoda lay in a pool of blood like a mop abandoned but still wet from unfinished business. John touched the dog's nose, felt the bullet hole in the shoulder, the broken bone. He found a fragment and turned it in his fingers. Creamy white, slippery. A flea hopped from Nikoda's body to John's weathered hand. It crawled up his wrist before jumping off again, before John had a chance to crush it like a stubborn seed.

October marked the sixth year since he had caught Nikoda in a trap. The trap had been set for muskrat down by the river, fifteen miles from the nearest house or farm, and concealed near the bank's edge beneath floating duckweed and an overhang of sedge grass. When John arrived on his morning check, he found an airedale puppy howling and trying to escape. It rattled the chain tied to a stake; bit stubbornly on the metal links.

He released the dog after deciding not to waste a bullet, but when it nipped and bit him in the forearms, reflected on his mistake. "Go home," he said. "Mangy mutt."

It hobbled and fell, yelped, then regained its footing to follow John home. It hopped on three legs and held the swollen paw off the ground.

"Don't think I'm feedin' you," he said, but the dog stayed with him despite mild threats and an occasional branch cartwheeling past its head. John gave up in the afternoon. While he split logs at the woodpile, the dog sat at a safe distance chewing wood chips into pulp.

That night the dog curled up near a big oak stump. John watched from the window and wondered if this was another intervention. The thing so puzzling to him was his belief that God usually took something—it was not His policy to give. "But for all I know," he thought, "the dog may be more trouble."

The next day near the woodpile John heard a bird calling above him; it sounded like "ni-ko-da, ni-ko-da," and he said it aloud.

The airedale was sniffing skunk odor in the fallen leaves. It pricked up its ears at the sound of John's voice.

"Nikoda," John said again, more loudly, and the dog ran over to him. "That's your name. If you ever had another—too bad."

The dog twisted its head wonderingly in the evening silence—when the birds stop singing, the wind dies, and the sun drops red behind darkening trees.

John would often sit outside in a patch of sunlight between the pines and scrape fat and oil from a pelt while Nikoda slept nearby in a scratched-out bed of dirt. When nothing bad resulted from the dog's presence, he started to believe God had finally tipped the scales in his favor and that his luck had changed as a reward for keeping faith.

John went outside to dig a hole. He dug down by the river where water rushing over rocks, bubbling under a dead and mossy branch, muffled the sound of the shovel's blade cutting earth and tree roots. He wrapped Nikoda in an old blanket and placed him in the grave as if the body was a chest of treasure he would some day return to and dig up again. He reached down and unwrapped the blanket from Nikoda, deciding he might need it for the winter, then covered the dog with fresh dirt.

"I known it," he said. "I should have shot you in the trap." He walked quietly through the trees back to the cabin.

"He enters my house, he kills my dog," John said. He lay on his bed and stared at the exposed beams with unplaned edges. He heard dry pine needles fall upon the roof. A small animal—a rat or squirrel—scurried across the tar paper; it made scratching noises with its tiny claws. "He enters my house, he kills my dog," he said again. Then he thought of something he had thought of before—when a bear had smashed and raided his smoke-house full of venison and when his Jeep sank to the axels in Brewer's Swamp—because it helped him live through trouble: The earth is the Lord's and the fullness thereof; the world, and they that dwell within.

Ed Philips drove back to his home—a small, two-room apartment built above the Texaco station at Four Corners. He parked next to a red canoe leaning against the station wall. It was a fiberglass sixteen-footer that Ed had not used for over a year. He could no longer carry it on his shoulders. The canoe's wooden yoke, a smooth strip of oak which balanced all the weight by being centrally placed between the gunwhales, pinched a nerve in the back of his neck and sent pains shooting down his crooked spine.

Ed relit his cigar, sucked the match flame inward. He limped past the yellow walls of the garage to a small entryway, up a narrow staircase with stubbornly high steps where a shadeless bulb, covered with dried wings and black specks, stuck out like a head of some exotic trophy above the door.

Inside, he hung his belt, holster, and handgun on a coat rack behind the door and made a sandwich and coffee. He heard a customer's car run over the signal hose before Frank Kopacki, the mechanic, ran out to give service. If it was not the signal hose ringing, it was Frank—coughing, dropping tools on the concrete, or singing hits by Johnny Cash.

"Hi. My name is *Sue*. How do you do!"

Ed did not feel like sleeping anyway. He paced the kitchen floor, cigar wedged between his lips, and shuffled back and forth with the left boot sliding a half step behind the right. He stopped suddenly as that singular, recurring notion hit him again: John Jenson had been jacking his deer for twenty years. "Damn hillbilly," he said. Grit from his boots scratched the linoleum. "He must be selling them—probably to some New York gangster."

He knew that old Sam Perk might overextend his trapline or during deer season some out-of-stater might mistake a billy goat for a spike-horned buck, but no one had less regard for the fish and game laws than Jenson. Ed's warnings were of less concern to him than a mouse rummaging through his grain bags. "He don't pay no attention to me," Ed said. He retied his boots in the hallway; crisscrossed the laces, pulled them snug. He was going to drive up Wells Road to the cornfield. He believed that Jenson would be there.

John dreamt that Nikoda was scratching on the front door. Instinctively he rose to let him in and remembered, at the latch, the warden holding his rifle and the glassy eye of the scope. Remembered Ed saying, Damn dog was a menace. Crazy mean.

Stars stretched across the clearing sky. Geese were flying overhead and honking. They often flew at night, safe from a gunner's blast—flew low over the pines, low enough for John to hear the beating of their wings. Might land in Owen's Pond, he thought. He listened to their calling fade and heard—no, he could not hear it—nothing. But the fresh dirt smell of a grave drifted in the air.

John walked past his Jeep, cut left into a pine grove where a prickly blanket of brown needles silenced his step. He walked beneath the sunless and dying lower limbs, beside the towering trunks, and thought about the pines growing throughout the winter months. Their shadows would cover the snow in blue, uneven spearhead shapes, while the maples and oaks stood dormant with naked branches—lifeless looking and yet still appearing to stretch, to get above the evergreens. But without those extra months to grow they could do no more than rattle against each other in a cold and closing sky.

John came to a clearing where two deer exploded from a laurel thicket, then vanished. He crossed an old logging trail, past the smooth gray bark of beeches. Upward, to the saddle where wind cut through a depression on a narrow ridge. He worked his way beyond familiar landmarks; climbed over boulders, near-vertical granite ledges covered with moss and fern or laid bare by erosion. He did not reach the mountain's summit until after midnight but, sitting on a boulder jutting out farther than the others, watched shooting stars arc across the sky. Then he said in a whisper: "That dog-murderin' bastard."

Ed Philips drove up Wells Road and backed his truck into the forest's edge near the cornfield. He had a hunch that Jenson would be out poaching tonight, trying to get even by shooting deer in the backcountry.

He sat in the truck with the lights out and radio turned off. He dozed off thinking of Jenson's way of looking beyond people—looking beyond Ed as if he wasn't there and never smiling at his jokes.

A droplet of sweat rolling down his neck awakened him. An unsettling sense of fear—from the darkness, from the quiet solitude?—made him tremble. He shook his head and shivered in the cold cab; his left leg was asleep. He pounded it against the floorboards.

The moon illuminated the field in half-light. The dry, gray stalks of corn rustled together in the wind. Ed imagined he heard something in the distance. He wondered if something was moving—walking. Toward him? It was not possible, he decided, to hear a man walk, especially if the man was across the field. And Jenson was too smart to make a noise like that. Maybe racoons were moving through the brush. Could someone be moving through the corn? It *was* Jenson, Ed thought, not caring about how much noise he made. Seething with rage at the warden for trespassing and killing the dog—walking unafraid across the field. Ed raised his rifle. Jenson was crazy with hatred. Crazy, like his dog. Ed snapped on the headlights and saw two glowing circles coming toward him. He fired, saw the smoke rise from the barrel, felt the walnut stock bury itself in his shoulder, and saw the body fall about thirty yards from the truck.

He got out slowly; worked the rifle bolt backward to eject the empty shell, then forward to push another bullet into the chamber.

A deer lay kicking feebly on the ground. Ed stared in disbelief. He had shot a small deer wandering out to feed on corn.

Two shots were fired past him as he stood above the wounded animal. His headlights shattered and left him in darkness. Another shot, then another, seemed directed at the truck. Flattening himself face down in the dirt, Ed heard the tires hiss like a cornered cat. The ground, he thought, felt warm—smelled rich of organic decay.

"Jenson?" he said. Ed raised his head up slightly, but another shot pinned him back down. "Don't kill me, please!"

The kicking sounds of the deer stopped. Sometimes the wind would rustle the corn and play tricks. He thought Jenson might be standing over him but did not dare look up to see.

"Jenson?" he said. Then he shouted, "Please, John! Let me go. It's getting cold. I'm older than you. The cold goes right through me sometimes. I don't care about the deer, I don't know anything about you . . ."

The aroma of soil filled his nostrils. It was sweet and fragrant and full of life. He began praying for his own life, mumbling about trying to be good.

He wondered if what he said was true; wondered if it was possible to pray face down without the words losing their effect or disappearing altogether into the ground.

John Jenson walked around the cornfield through an early morning fog. An orange glow was burning through the haze from beyond a black wall of trees. The truck was parked in a thicket of blackberries, and the warden lay in a fallow strip of earth which ran beside the last row of corn. John prodded Ed to roll over on his back. Dirt stuck to his face. Not daring to look Jenson in the eyes, Ed looked up and away as if watching for geese in the sky.

John knew that if the geese were flying now they would be flying high above the haze and no one would see them; he at least might know that they were there.

"Don't ever go in my house when I ain't home," he said. He poked Ed with the rifle barrel. "Hey!—You hear me?"

"Yes."

"Swear it."

"Please don't kill me."

"Swear you won't go in my house!"

"I swear to God." Ed shivered uncontrollably.

"You better get going and ask Frank for a tow." John walked away from the warden and over to the deer. He pulled his knife from its sheath and slit the belly open from ass to rib cage. When he turned, Ed was sitting up and watching.

"What the hell you lookin' at?" John said.

"Nothin'."

"Nothin'? Ain't you watching me gut this deer?"

"I don't see nothin'."

John put the severed tongue into his plastic bag. "Well, I'm cleanin' a gut-shot deer, and the guy who shot it ought to be ashamed. Ashamed every day of his life."

Ed got up and brushed the dirt from his pants. He walked toward the road, then he turned to look once more at Jenson. Only the rut marks remained, uneven and deeply branded in the soil, where John had already dragged the deer into the trees.

Being Right and Being Wrong

According to the formula, all showdowns take place at high noon or at sunset, and the good guy always wins. There are two showdowns in "The Field." Both of them happen at night, and it is hard to say who should win.

John Jenson has a simple value system: he lets God decide the bigger issues, and he lets common-sense principles decide the rest. The way Jenson sees it, God either gives or He takes away. Situations are either good or bad. The problem is that Ed Philips, the game warden, also follows a simple philosophy: the law is the law. And he is paid to enforce it.

Why do the shootouts in "The Field" take place on dark nights instead of in bright sunlight? One reason might be to show that principles and philosophy and law are often not clear; morals and fairness and justice are seldom clear-cut issues. Who has the most right to make rules for the field—the man who takes his living from it, or the man who is hired to enforce the hunting regulations?

Jenson is a "wiry," strong, and self-reliant character. His philosophy of life is much the same—tough and individualistic. Philips, on the other hand, is a pale, fat, twisted, and dissatisfied character. But does being strong and independent give Jenson the right to poach deer? Should we approve of the way he beats the law, just because the law is represented by a man we don't like?

The story provides the answer in the last scene, when Philips asks Jenson what he is doing, and Jenson replies, "I'm cleanin' a gut-shot deer, and the guy who shot it ought to be ashamed. Ashamed every day of his life."

Why should he be ashamed? Ashamed of what? Jenson's words puzzled me at first. Then I realized what he meant: he may have forgotten other distinctions in life, such as the sex of a deer he has shot, but he is keenly aware of the difference between shooting humans for revenge and shooting animals for food. Unlike Philips, Jenson would never try to avenge his insulted pride by shooting a man from ambush.

Mark Holden's story is a long way from being a formula gunfight; however, it still illustrates the difference—or at least one of the differences—between being right and being wrong. As Holden said in a recent letter, "My work has its origins in my personal experience as a bowhunter, and the notion of an Authority with little or no moral principle imposing regulations and laws on a lawless, but highly principled man."